Praise for Michael Gerber and
A CHRISTMAS PERIL

"A parody of Dickens' *A Christmas Carol*? Sure, like nobody's ever thought of *that*."

—Sy Lentnite, *Scranton Globe-Globe*

"Back in 1843 when the original story was appeared, the traditions of Christmas were in decline. Some believe that Dickens' ghostly little tale of redemption actually created the holiday we celebrate today.

A Christmas Peril, on the other hand, just might kill it."

—O. Tannenbaum, *Commonwhelp*

"I'll give this book one thing: it's short."

—Steve Allen, deceased

BY THIS AUTHOR

PARODIES
Barry Trotter and the Unauthorized Parody
Barry Trotter and the Unnecessary Sequel
Barry Trotter and the Dead Horse
The Chronicles of Blarnia

NOVELS
Freshman
Sophmore

ESSAYS
Our Kampf (with Jonathan Schwarz)

• • •

Watch for my new comic novel starring John Lennon
(with and without The Beatles)
COMING 2009!

A
CHRISTMAS
PERIL

Mr. Fezziwig's Balls Chafed.

A CHRISTMAS PERIL.

A PARODY.

BEING

What Happened Next.

BY

MICHAEL GERBER.

ORIGINAL ILLUSTRATIONS GLEEFULLY DESECRATED.

SANTA MONICA.
CUCKOO BOOKS, LLC.

MMVIII.

Additional copies can be ordered via Amazon.com;
for bulk orders, contact the author at mikegerber.com.
Other inquiries may be made
c/o McIntosh and Otis,
353 Lexington Ave., NY, NY 10016.

First edition, for whatever *that's* worth
Printed in the United States of America

Reinforced binding. DO NOT EAT.
The Library of Congress has pointedly ignored this book,
and can you blame them?

ISBN 1-890470-05-8

Merry Christmas!

TABLE OF CONTENTS.

———•———

*Illustrations
sprinkled throughout.*

A CHRISTMAS PERIL.

STAVE I.

SCREW-AGE.

UPON THE existence of ghosts, reasonable people may differ; and in the matter of Ebenezer Scrooge they certainly did. One clique of disbelievers was certain he had suffered a minor stroke, while another faction pointed to the mind-altering properties of some of the food additives found in your less-reputable taverns. But on one point there was no disagreement: Scrooge was a changed man.

Overnight, the miser had become a firehose of generosity, spraying good works and good fellowship forcefully in every direction. No one could escape his hoarse shouts of "Merry Christmas!" which lasted until March (and began again in October), nor could they ignore the rictus-like smile which hung across his features like so much brittle and decaying holiday garland. "Merry Christmas! Happy Easter! Good Kissing Friday! I'm sending you a fat goose whether you want one or not!"

No one was safe from this relentless two-legged cornucopia: In the daytime, Scrooge doled out large sums at his counting-house, and in the nights, he walked London's neighborhoods, flinging coin like a farmer broadcasts seed. Were there injuries? To be sure—but Scrooge kept up his manic charity. After all, didn't his very soul depend upon it?

Decent people avoided the new Scrooge. They believed in the wisdom of our ancestors as regards leopards and spots. What good was it for the new Scrooge to gift them a pound, if the old Scrooge demanded it back—with interest? Surely Scrooge's old ways would return. Surely the old miser-mind still crouched in Scrooge's brainpan, waiting to ooze forth at the moment of maximum injury!

But it did not. By the next Christmas Eve, the sacred, crazy spark inside Scrooge burned more brightly than ever. This was excellent news for London's baser sort, who circled the old man like sharks, drawn by the penetrating scent of free money.

No mountebank collecting funds for a fake orphanage, no gambler swaddling his losses in a tale of blameless woe, no "widow" with malnutrition makeup and a rented child neglected to pay a visit to Ebenezer Scrooge. Once there, no gambit was too brazen for them, secure in the knowledge that their payday had been vouchsafed by a collection of bullying spirits. For while Scrooge had changed, the world around him had not; and the dark impulses that impel the wicked to pray upon the good remained as strong as ever.

Scrooge knew this, but tried not to let it bother him overmuch. He embraced his new profession with the same single-mindedness that had once made him pinch every penny until the copper smudged his fingers. Where Scrooge had once accumulated, he now disbursed. And he was good at it, too—he even advertised.

"Short of Cash? Money Troubles Making Life
Too Much to Bear?
Come See **EBENEZER SCROOGE**, Benefactor to the World!
No Want Too Small! <u>No One</u> Turned Down!
Scrooge & Cratchit (Formerly Scrooge & Marley)
Near the Stock Exchange
Don't Wait! Apply Today!"

Scrooge had put into practice every lesson the spirits had imparted. The only trouble was that one side of the ledger held all the world's misery, while the other side contained only Scrooge, and no man, no matter how well-intentioned, could reconcile that account.

And so, at the twelve-month anniversary of his transformation, Ebenezer Scrooge was exhausted. His features were drawn, his wrinkles deeper. His eyes were bloodshot, his tongue was coated, and his hair was falling out. If Scrooge's circulation was bad—and it was!—his digestion was even worse; most foodstuffs transited his quailing system practically whole. Scrooge's movements were slow and clumsy; his thinking, muddy and erratic. And to top it all off, Scrooge took even less care with his appearance now than before—moments spent combing his hair or blinking or using a handkerchief were moments lost to his greater goal.

The goal was great, there was no doubt about that—just ask the supplicants jammed into Scrooge's counting house! In a small waiting room outside Scrooge's office, a mass of humanity clamored and writhed, wreathed in wretchedness, profanity, and stink. They jostled against Scrooge's door, pounding on it when he took too long, kicking it when they were angry. There was no getting past the grasping, chanting, many-armed mass—they'd frequently lift Scrooge up and rifle his pockets, providing the reason for the old man's "charity" only after they'd taken the coins. Scrooge had to climb out of the window just to get his lunch.

Today he was unlucky; Scrooge had slipped on the sill and toppled into a snowbank below. No one had bothered to help—last-minute shoppers scurried oblivious through the midday murk, and even the children, whom one might expect to be slightly more sensible to the sentiments of the season, had merely pointed and laughed. One, a pug-nosed urchin with a prominent wen, had tossed a stone at him. It was standard treatment; kids teased Scrooge all the time, following him in a pack demanding money, and swearing at him when he ran out.

Now, four hours later, Scrooge rubbed the knee he'd wrenched. The old man tried to concentrate on the deranged charwoman babbling out her dreams in front of him.

"I aim to dust the entire world," the woman said in a sing-song particular to the mentally ill. Not that Scrooge needed the extra clue; she was as smudgy as a chimney sweep, and as she talked, she danced an unspeakably grimy duster over Scrooge's desk and environs.

"Go on." Scrooge tried to listen, really he did, but after a while all the stories sounded the same. His mind wandered...Perhaps the spirits would visit the pug-nosed boy tonight...Let's see him chuck a rock at the Ghost of Christmas to Come! The old man chuckled to himself at the thought of it.

"Is there something funny about dusting the entire world?" the charwoman demanded.

"No, no, Mrs. Speckle," Scrooge lied. "It was a hiccup."

"Well," she said prickily, "don't interrupt. It's rude."

"I'm sorry," Scrooge said. "Please continue."

"What did I just say about interrupting?" She flicked her duster at him.

Scrooge smiled silently, hoping Mrs. Speckle wouldn't become violent. It happened frequently, and was no wonder; in a society where money is the only measure, it is only natural that the needy resent their benefactors most of all. Scrooge knew this, and tried to forbear, but did not relish the prospect of another pocketbook across the face. If it came to that, there was really no place to escape—Mrs. Speckle sat between him and the window.

The offices, always cramped, now held three chambers instead of two; and since it seemed wrong to inconvenience Mr. Cratchit, the waiting room had come out of Scrooge's portion. Now he did not have an office as much as a closet. Small as it was, this little room saw exceedingly heavy traffic: One hundred visitors a day was usual, and two hundred was not unheard of. On this day—Christmas Eve, as I have said—the flow of customers had become a torrent. Some were feeling the pinch incurred by that most expensive of holidays, while others were convinced the anniversary would make Scrooge even more generous than usual.

"I want five pounds," the hard-faced Mrs. Speckle said, naming the highest figure she could conceive. They all did.

Scrooge felt a pang. Five pounds could buy enough rotgut to float a ship of the line. If this was simply a gambit to enrich a local pub, the poor sot would be frozen stiff in Regent's Park within the week. Still, the spirits had tasked him to serve, not to judge...

"Very reasonable indeed," Scrooge lied, unlocking his desk and extracting some coins. "After all, it is the entire world."

Mrs. Speckle didn't answer, busy counting her windfall. Then the greed lighting her broad, grimy features dimmed with concern. "What if I need more?" she croaked.

"Just come back," Scrooge said, sure he would never see her again. In the unlikely event that her ambitions were genuine, her days were just as numbered. As a rule, dear reader, the world's wild animals do not wish to be dusted, and respond intemperately towards anyone who attempts to do so.

"No need to thank me, Mrs. Speckle," Scrooge said, guiding the calico-covered maniac towards the door. "It is my belief we were put on this earth to help one another."

"You don't have to get all high and mighty about it," Mrs. Speckle said, flicking her duster at him.

Hand on the doorknob, Scrooge felt a particle crater into his right eyeball. Shutting his eye tightly against the searing pain, Scrooge opened his heart even wider. He knew Mrs. Speckle's condition wasn't her fault, any more than his miserdom had been. Who knew what malign Fate had forged the freak waddling beside him? "All I ask, Mrs. Speckle, is this: if you ever have an opportunity to help someone else…"

"Someone else?" the smudgy dynamo suddenly screeched. "There's *someone else* aiming to dust the entire world?"

"No, no, no, most assuredly not." Scrooge spoke in soothing tones, but edged towards the window just in case.

"Tell me who it is! I'll *kill* her!"

"Calm down, Mrs. Speckle. Deep breaths." Scrooge knew that flattery was the Achilles heel of the monomaniac, and poured it on. "I only meant, if you meet someone doing something else equally worthy—as if such an activity could possibly exist—consider helping them as I have helped you. Now, go: fulfill your great destiny."

As soon as Scrooge opened the door, a mass of bodies heaved forward. People began to shout.

"I'm next, Mr. Scrooge!"

"Don't listen to her, Scroogie—I'm next!"

"You godd—d son of a w—e, give me some money or I'll gut you!"

Scrooge smiled—things always got a little hostile near closing time. "Last of the day!" he called out mildly. These words were the signal for a vast brawl.

This, too, was usual. Scrooge closed the door. He looked out of the window as he waited patiently for the violence to take its course. As something heavy thunked against the door—almost certainly a skull—Scrooge noticed it was snowing again.

When the cries and tumult died down, Scrooge stepped back to the door and opened it. A bloodied pair of victors waded out of the tangle of broken humanity: a clergyman and his African ward.

"They cut in line!" someone yelled weakly.

"Good afternoon, gentlemen," Scrooge said, offering them each a handkerchief to staunch their various wounds. Then Scrooge extended his hand in friendship and welcome.

"Chief Oobu-Joobu don't shake. 'e thinks it steals 'is soul," the clergyman said, shaking Scrooge's hand. "Kype's the name. Reverend Phineas Kype." Kype chewed a toothpick as he talked, and his eight knuckles bore the words "Love" and "'ate" tattooed on them, one letter each. He turned to the Chief. "SCROOGE," Kype said loudly, jabbing a sausage-like finger at the ex-miser. "'IM GOOD MAN."

"MONEY ME!" the Chief said, thumping his chest.

"In a moment, Chief." Greed truly knew no nationality. Scrooge turned back to the man of God. "So you're some sort of...?"

"Bloke what goes an' 'elps out...You know, in darkest Africa."

"I see," Scrooge said, inwardly impressed with the creativity. He decided to have a little fun. "I've never been to darkest Africa. What's it like?"

"Erm...well..." The clergyman began to perspire. Several seconds ticked by.

"*Dark*, perhaps?"

14

Kype seized upon this with gratitude. "Oh, yeh! Very dark."

"Incredibly dark," the Chief chimed in.

"So he knows English?" Scrooge asked.

"Just a few phrases," Kype said sweatily.

"You got lucky," the Chief said.

"That one, too," Kype said, striking his companion lightly on the back of the noggin. "Anyway, Africa's so dark, you can 'ardly see your 'and in fronta your face."

"Really?" Scrooge said. If these people would put one-tenth the effort into actual jobs...

"Oh, yeh! The natives there aren't black—they're bruised. From bumpin' inna things."

The Chief mimed bumping into something comically, then smiled broadly.

Scrooge smiled back. "Tell me," he asked, "did you see the Eiffel Tower when you were there?"

Kype drew another blank.

"Come, now," Scrooge said. "Surely you saw it. It's world-famous."

"Oh, that Eiffel Tower," Kype said. "I thought you were talkin' about the other one. 'Course we did." Kype jabbed a thumb towards the Chief. "'e practically lives in it."

"Does he? That's very interesting, since"—Scrooge applied the cat's paw— "the Eiffel Tower isn't in Africa. It is in Paris, France!"

There was another embarrassed silence.

Finally, Chief Oobu-Joobu spoke. "But gov—it's only 1844. The Eiffel Tower won't be built for another forty years."

"Don't try to change the subject," Scrooge said. "Reverend Kype, I know you're not a real missionary. In fact, I'd wager you've never traveled farther south than Brighton."

"Not even," the Chief said with a chuckle, but Kype feigned indignation. "'ow dare you, Mr. Scrooge! Insultin' a man of the cloth!"

"A man made from whole-cloth, perhaps...Since when does the

C of E tattoo 'Born to Raise 'ell' upon people's necks?" Scrooge reached over and dabbed at the Chief's cheek, then presented his blackened fingertip. "Boot blacking," he said. "And 'Oobu-Joobu'? That's just silly. Come on, fellows—even a life of crime requires a modicum of effort."

"'e made it up, I swear!" the Chief said, pointing to Kype. "Don't turn us in, gov—I've got a wife and two babes."

"I highly doubt it," Scrooge said. "But I am not here to judge. Judging's for a higher authority." He opened the desk, then tossed them each a coin. "Here's a guinea. Merry Christmas."

Their eyes lit up with the myriad perversions that could be inaugurated for such a princely sum. "Thanks!"

"Now go, and sin no more," Scrooge said.

"We won't," they lied.

"I believe you," Scrooge lied back.

The waiting room was empty now, save for some sticks of broken furniture, and the bodies of the injured. Scrooge sighed—what a sight for Christmas Eve. But then again, it was Christmas Eve, and nothing could be wholly bad on that day. This brightened Scrooge considerably, and he whistled as he hauled the ruined chairs and tables out into the snow.

He was endeavoring to revive the sundry unconscious (after, of course, slipping tuppence into their unknowing pockets) when the front door burst open. Scrooge grabbed a weapon, fearing that Speckle had returned—but it was only Fred, Scrooge's nephew.

"Merry Christmas, Uncle!" he boomed. Never did these words exit his lips without rattling windows.

Scrooge straightened—at his age, not a painless process—and returned Fred's salutation. In Scrooge's estimation, Fred seemed half in the bag. And so he was; in those difficult times, dear reader, ones so much less diverting than our own, it was the custom to walk around in a constant state of semi-inebriation. This is an essential fact, and nothing in the story that I am about to relate makes much sense at all unless you believe it. Who sees ghosts? Who is prone to sudden, violent shifts of behavior? In this story, as in the first one, the wise reader must assume that every character is more or less drunk.

At the moment, however, Scrooge was basically sober. "Would you give me an early present and help me get this gentleman up and about?" It was well past dark, and Scrooge wanted to eat and get to bed, as well as remedy that sobriety I just mentioned.

Unfortunately, in addition to being the family's original Christmas freak, Fred had been born with a deep and abiding horror of gainful employ. He considered any form of purposeful activity as the first step down a slippery slope. So he demurred.

"Gee, Uncle, I'd love to," Fred said, "but I've got this dreadfully frayed cuticle..."

"Right," Scrooge sighed. Since he had opened his coffers, his nephew had become even lazier than before; and that wife of Fred's was no better—she had just hired a servant to breathe for her. "Then can I prevail upon you, Fred, to go outside and get me

Scrooge often worked off excess stress by manhandling traffic cones.

a handful of snow? It might numb your injury."

Fred assumed an expression of pained remorse. "Normally I would, but—"

"Forget it! Forget it!" Scrooge said, exasperated. He dashed outside—it was bitter cold—and scooped up a handful of the soot-streaked snow. Back in the waiting room, he pressed it against the faces of the unconscious people, to wake them up. Then Scrooge fished a gold sovereign out of his pocket, and showed it around. "Attention, everyone! I'm going to throw this outside, and whoever finds it first, gets to keep it."

"Excellent!" Fred said. As lazy as he was, free money always invigorated him. Limbering up, he looked around at the injured. "You blighters are going *down!*"

"Not you, Fred." Scrooge opened the door, and tossed out the coin. The waiting room emptied like a shot. "The lame walk," Scrooge said. "It's a miracle."

"A Christmas miracle," Fred said. "Anyway, I was in the neighborhood, Uncle, picking up a thing or seven for the wife, and—"

"—you needed a little extra money?"

"Now that you mention it," Fred said good-humoredly. "Trust me, Uncle: you did right not to marry. It's ruinously expensive!"

Especially with your wife, Scrooge thought, imagining that dimple-creased, bow-bedecked monster with an involuntary shudder. Our virtues and faults, dear reader, often issue from the same sources, and Fred's partner was no exception. Scrooge's niece-by-marriage was an attractive woman, some might say too much so; and while that made her unquestionably delightful to look at, it also made her a perfect hell to live with. For as surely as she turned gentlemen's heads, Fred's wife carried the curse of her sort: vanity. Everything she owned had to be as pleasing and rare as her many suitors said *she* was; only then could Fred's wife be momentarily content. And valuable things were necessary, too, to cushion the day when her beauty was gone. Her looks were all she had—there never walked a woman less equipped to exist upon her virtues, nor less willing to try.

Fred's wife knew this, and the thought of a penniless future filled her with dread. She was preparing to abandon Fred for a man of better prospects (or possibly just a Bank) when Scrooge's metamorphosis took place. The softening of Scrooge's heart filled her own breast with hope—hope of prying as much money out of her husband's Uncle as possible.

At first she tried the direct approach, but the old man proved uninterested in the pleasures of the flesh. Her present tactic— making Fred wheedle for cash—was a temporary measure, as she weighed various options up to and including murder. To give her husband's wheedling maximum urgency, Fred's wife had instituted monthly target amounts, and drove her mate ruthlessly. There was even a thermometer illustration in their kitchen, which Mrs. Fred colored in whenever her husband brought home more of Scrooge's money.

With a supreme effort, Scrooge drove the nasty Mrs. Fred from his mind. He slid open his desk drawer and asked his nephew, "How much do you need?"

"Oh...not much," Fred said, then with a studied casualness named a figure that made Scrooge briefly lose consciousness.

Fred saw the flutter. "Uncle Scrooge! Are you all right?" he asked, instantly calculating the bequest.

"Yes, yes," Scrooge said, rummaging through the coins. "Only I don't think I have that much on-hand."

"Whatever you've got is close enough," Fred said. He'd become much more brazen of late; Fred's wife had announced that there would be no physical affection between them until her Draconian targets had been met.

"Open your pocket," Scrooge said, then filled the right one until it bulged like a tumor.

"Top it off, top it off. It can take more."

As he filled the other, Scrooge said, "Fred, I can't keep doing this. I must help those in need."

"I *am* in need," Fred said, hopping up and down so more coins could fit. "I'm *desperate*." His cobwebbed groin throbbed plaintively in silent agreement.

"No, you don't want to get a job," Scrooge said. "There's a difference."

Fred scowled. "Out of all London," he complained, "should I alone be unable to call on your generosity simply because I'm your flesh and blood? Forgive me for saying so, dear Uncle," Fred said, "but that is f—d up. Our relation should give me more claim, not less. And I alone have shown affection for you regardless of your generosity. Remember how nice I was to you last year, when you were still despised by all?"

"I wasn't despised," Scrooge said. "Disliked, perhaps, misunderstood—"

"Pish and tosh!" Fred said. "People were burning you in effigy, and on the hottest days of the year! Yet I wished you 'Merry Christmas.' I even invited you to dinner!"

"I remember—you make sure I do," Scrooge said. "Still, it is true you have been kind to me and I appreciate it. But even you must admit that your wife cannot say the same."

"Oh, Uncle, you'll like her better in time," Fred lied. He certainly hadn't. In fact, the money in his pocket was going towards an Escape Fund. When Fred reached a certain plateau, he planned to hop a ship for Italy and never return. Let her shift for herself, the rouge-caked trollop. "My wife merely hides her affections—as you used to, Uncle."

Scrooge grunted.

Fred swallowed nervously. Grunting was uncomfortably close to Scrooge's old manner; could he be slipping back? Fred wondered. He changed the subject. "Tell me, Uncle: how many of God's creatures did you help today?"

"Let's see," Scrooge said, beginning to dress for the cold walk home. "Someone trying to start a fake orphanage, three widows with rented children, a raft of girls about to give birth to pillows, some gamblers, some degenerates..."

"Stop, stop! Before my view of humanity darkens to blindness!"

"Welcome to my world," Scrooge said, with a wan smile. "The spirits didn't tell me about the crooks. Or the crazies."

"Of course they didn't. They probably work on commission."

Scrooge had finished putting on his coat. Next to the coat tree sat a large parcel wrapped in brown paper. ""Oh, I also got a bronze bust from the Prince of Wales."

"Uncle! We must celebrate!" Fred exclaimed, angling for a better dinner than he would get at home. (His wife's legions of servants, though full of boy-toys and gossip-buddies, did not include one decent cook.) "Let us toast the royal gift!"

Scrooge deflected this suggestion, wishing to eat alone and turn in early. "I'm not sure it was meant in esteem," he said. "They gave it to me as a bribe. Apparently I've given so much money, inflation is skyrocketing throughout the Empire."

"Well," Fred said, "that s—ks, if you don't mind my saying so." He looked at the object. "It is the very image of you."

"Looks rather crosseyed to me...Fred, could you help—"

Fred had a special horror of anything heavy. "Oh, my lord, no!" he exclaimed with a laugh. "Uncle, are you mad?"

"Thought not. Just being optimistic, since it's Christmas..." Scrooge leaned down and picked up the package, feeling several essential internal structures give way. "I was just hoping...after I gave you all that money..."

"Uncle, it's precisely that money which prevents me from helping," Fred said, patting his distended thighs. "I'm loaded to the gunwales as it is. Any more effort, and I might swamp. Anyway, I'm the one doing you a favor. You had to give me that money, otherwise"—Fred wiggled his fingers—"'crackle, crackle, crackle!'"

Scrooge was annoyed. Everybody knows I have to give them money. And yet they have to give me nothing in return! "No matter how much I give, it's never enough!" he muttered.

Fred, naturally, saw none of his own behavior in this remark, only an opportunity to enrich himself further. "Uncle, you know I support your new generosity. But you are being used by all these strangers. What about spreading joy and affection within one's own family? For one thing, there are fewer of us, so it's bound to be cheaper!"

"Doesn't seem very cheap."

Fred slapped Scrooge on the back jovially, nearly toppling him. "Better hope the spirits aren't listening, you old grouch!" he teased, silently heaping another blessing on those spectral bullies. "Have you done any shopping? What will you do for Christmas? Will you come over for dinner again? We so enjoyed your company last year—especially the wife." This was a lie; Fred's wife had ritualistically destroyed everything Scrooge had touched, eaten from, or sat on.

"There's no time," Scrooge said. "Tomorrow is a 'wandering day.'" This was Scrooge's term for treading the streets of London, forcing money on anything vaguely sentient. "I would dine with you, Fred, but I must think of my immortal soul. I have so many years to make up for, so much meanness to expunge."

"Easy, Uncle." Fred oozed faux-concern. "You'll blow a boiler. One man can only hold so much grace...Ready for the cold?"

Fred's hand was on the knob, but Scrooge bade him stop. The ex-miser rested the bust on a splintered end-table, then commenced digging through his coat pockets. "Must leave a few farthings for the mice—"

"Oh, Uncle," Fred said, "rodents don't even *use* money."

"These ones do."

"Then you've spoiled them," Fred said sternly. "Uncle, you must measure your charity, giving where it makes the most good. It's not enough to give—one must give wisely."

"The spirits didn't say anything about that," Scrooge said.

"It was implied," Fred said. "Go home. Rest. Then come over for dinner."

"The last time I did, your wife's cooking made me violently ill. I think she was trying to poison me."

She probably was, Fred thought. "So bring your own food."

Bob Cratchit leaned out of his office, a wave of delicious heat rolling forth. "Mr. Scrooge," he said, fixing his employer with a gaze slightly unfocused by strong drink, "I wonder if I might have a word with you?"

"Of course, Bob. I see you've started celebrating early." Scrooge pointed to the umbrella-bedecked tiki mug in Bob's right hand.

Cratchit was shirtless, and his skin bore the reddish hue that comes from prolonged exposure to a roaring blaze. He noticed Scrooge was not alone.

"Fred," he said icily.

"Bob," Fred answered, the smallish syllable packed with hate.

Ever since Scrooge's transformation, the two men had fought for control of the old man's affections, like dogs tussling over a beefsteak. It was an even fight: While the former was a blood relation, Cratchit was now Scrooge's partner in the counting house, and tended to all the business that Scrooge, preoccupied as he was with matters of income redistribution, could not.

"Any new business today, Bob?" Scrooge asked.

"No, sir," Cratchit said. There hadn't been any for months. Vastly immature, Cratchit had always been much more interested in play than work. At first, he contented himself with long lunches, then extended vacations, which he filled playing blind-man's-buff and other insipid contests. But eventually the local urchins had tired of the man-child's company, and barred him from their games. Forced to stay at work, an angry Cratchit had embarked on a campaign to alienate all of Scrooge's old clients, as well as discourage any new ones; happily, this gambit was totally successful.

Now with his days blessedly free and Scrooge a ridiculously easy touch, the ex-wretch had turned his formerly bone-chilling office into a Caribbean fantasia, complete with palm trees and a sand floor. Maintaining a constant temperature of 85 degrees Fahrenheit took so much coal that the plume stretched into the ionosphere. It had become a London landmark. On a clear day, you could see it from Belgium.

"I'd like to hire a steel band," Cratchit said.

Scrooge looked at Fred, who looked cross. "Uncle, charity

begins at home," he whisper-snarled.

"Erm, perhaps after Christmas, Bob," Scrooge said. "Surely we can get them cheaper then?"

Cratchit wasn't ready to give up yet. "But it would spread so much joy!"

A vein had emerged from Fred's temple. He grabbed the thing nearest to hand—a piece of that afternoon's mail—and began mauling it with great thoroughness.

Scrooge got the message. "I don't think so, Bob..."

Cratchit wheeled out his big gun. "But Mr. Scrooge, my son Tim specifically asked for it...You remember Tim? The"—Cratchit paused for effect—"cripple?"

"Oh, dirty pool!" Fred exclaimed.

Cratchit ignored him. "It was to be Tim's only present. You know how he never thinks of himself, only of others."

Right on cue, Scrooge began to trickle.

"I know it's a lot, but it would mean so much...to Tim." Cratchit poured it on. "After all, we don't know how many more Christmases he'll have..."

Scrooge burst into tears. The bust hit the floor with a clang. "What is the admiration of the Prince of Wales," he exclaimed, "compared to the love of one little boy?" He hugged Cratchit, getting suntan lotion all over the front of his coat. "Forgive me, Bob—what was I thinking? Hire the musicians immediately. And tell Tim *they're from me.*"

Fred threw down his handfuls of half-shredded mail in disgust. Everyone but Scrooge knew that Tiny Tim, a/k/a "Master T.," was now the head of one of London's top criminal gangs—and that Scrooge's sentimental largesse formed the very foundation of his unholy empire.

"I shall." Mid-hug, Cratchit looked over Scrooge's shoulder and stuck his tongue out. This was too much for Scrooge's nephew to bear. "Uncle, Mr. Cratchit is taking advantage of you."

"Oh, Fred, you believe everyone is taking advantage of me," Scrooge said, still speaking into Cratchit's sunburned pectorals.

Cratchit pulled away from his boss. "Fred, I can't believe you would say such a thing."

"The state of your office alone suggests that I must," Fred said. "My God, man—is that a pelican?"

"Which I am nursing back to health! For the London Zoo!" Cratchit said indignantly. He turned to his employer. "The poor animal was—those of us without money must tend to our immortal souls in other ways."

"Good, Bob," Scrooge said. "The spirits would be proud of you."

"Oh, s—d the spirits!" Fred said.

"Fred!" Scrooge was appalled; Cratchit was delighted. To impugn the spirits—this *had* to spell the end of Fred as a rival. But before Scrooge could lay into his nephew, a lithe woman with Asian features and a coconut-shell bra leaned out of the doorway.

"The coconut oil is warmed, Mister Robert. It is time for your rubdown..."

"In a moment," Cratchit said quickly, then saw the look Fred was giving him. "She's my sister," he explained.

"B—s," Fred mumbled.

"FRED!" Scrooge said angrily. "If you do not show Mr. Cratchit a little Christmas cheer, I swear by every spirit, I'll cut your hourly allowance in half!"

"What do the spirits say about employees hiding two sacks of unanswered correspondence under their back porches?"

"That's a lie!" Cratchit said, splitting hairs. There were actually four sacks.

"Fred, I am ashamed of you! You're asking for a visit tonight, truly you are," Scrooge said. "We'll discuss it later."

"Yes, Uncle," Fred said, "we most assuredly will." Fred jammed his hat onto his head, yanked open the front door, and stomped out into the swirling snow.

"See you tomorrow for dinner! I'll bring the goose!"

Fred turned. "Merry Christmas!" he shouted with maximum irony. As he did so, Fred was nearly run down by Tiny Tim's massive, pimped-out omnibus.

"Get outta the road, yeh freak!" Master T's scabby driver Crippen yelled.

Scrooge picked up the bust once again.

"What's in there?" Cratchit asked. "A present?"

"Of sorts," Scrooge said. "The Prince of Wales gave it to me, in hopes of keeping me from donating to anything in the coming year. Apparently it demoralizes the other donors."

"You must be proud," Cratchit said.

"Sure. But it won't stop me," Scrooge said, smiling. "The spirits made it clear: I have a job to do, Bob, and I can't stop until either everyone is happy or all my money's gone."

"That's the spirit!" Cratchit said, delighted. Then the clerk added in his most honeyed voice, "You know, we meant to get you a present, Mr. Scrooge…"

"Don't worry about it, Bob. That's not what Christmas is about."

"I know," Cratchit said. "You of all people have proven that. It's just that a groat doesn't go as far as it used to. There's all the kids…And Tim's artificial spleen. It's made of Sumatran manganese…"

"I wanted to ask how that worked out," Mr. Scrooge said. "I apologize for being so callous."

"It's functioning perfectly, Mr. Scrooge. Though it may need some expensive new parts in the coming year."

"I stand at the ready, Bob. Well," Scrooge said, stepping outside, "a very Merry Christmas to you, and to all the other Cratchits. The goose is from me, of course—and whatever else you require. I've opened accounts in your name at every grocer in Camden Town, so don't be stingy with yourself, Bob!"

"Thank you, Mr. Scrooge! Merry Christmas!" Still bare-chested, Cratchit closed the door quickly. His smile faded the moment the door closed, and was replaced by a worried expression which did not fade. Fred had threatened his gravy train before, but this time it was more serious. He'd have to keep a very close eye on that fellow—

"Mister Robert?" the voluptuous native-girl called from inside his office. "Aren't you coming for your 'happy ending'?"

—but first, Bob needed a massage!

Scrooge disapproved of Marley's bondage gear.

STAVE TWO.

———•———

INTO THE SOUP.

By a quirk of London's topography, the region which contained Scrooge's office—as well as his chambers, some distance away—was a natural bowl, so that all the smoke and fog in the city collected there. This made getting around difficult, somewhat like swimming through gruel. On particularly bad evenings, when the atmosphere was positively viscous, the inhabitants were wont to employ small, hand-sized shovels to speed their progress by digging a sort of passage, or channel, through the air as they walked. This night was particularly difficult going, with Nature adding her own frosty ingredients to the particulated stew.

Scrooge didn't mind this inconvenience a bit, as it ensured that this neighborhood was the cheapest in London. Frugality was still a watchword for him: before his skirmish with the spirits, Scrooge insisted his money stay securely in the bank. After, he tried to keep his expenses to a minimum, to maximize his charity.

With the bust tucked under one arm and the scent of Bob Cratchit's suntan oil still wafting from his overcoat, Scrooge trudged through the sooty snow. He shoveled with his right hand, but it did no good. The air was especially hefty this evening, and while that meant slow going, it also made things distinctly safer for the brittle-boned ex-miser; anyone who happened to slip on a patch of ice would fall quite gently, gravity being offset by the pudding-like quality of the vapors. On the way down, Scrooge had had enough time to wonder if other holidays boasted a contingent of spirits. Were excessively mild people visited on Halloween, and exhorted to be scarier? Were prudes rousted from their beds on St. Valentine's Day? And what was *their* lesson? Scrooge blushed to think of it.

It may surprise you, dear reader, to know that the reformed Scrooge took his evening meal in the same melancholy tavern as he had exactly twelve months before. First, it was close to his office, a signal virtue on a teeth-chattering night like this. Second, it was cheap—and we have already discussed Scrooge's views on that subject. And, third, habits of the stomach are even more difficult to change than habits of the heart—even if, as in this case, they put the bearer in quite a bit of danger.

Danger? Certainly. On Christmas Eve? That night above all others. Christmas can be a bitter experience, a time when what one lacks, or has lost, looms larger than any current blessing. There's a reason why the suicides go up.

As we have seen, Scrooge's activity had attracted a sizeable portion of the criminal element to the precincts of his office; and after such an influx, it was only natural that the shops and restaurants there would begin to cater to this roughest trade.

The aim of Scrooge's tavern, The Ball and Chain, was to put its customers in a spending mood by reminding them of home— "home" in this case being Newgate Prison. With depressing décor, an alarming clientele, and truly execrable food, The Ball and Chain did a brisk business—mostly due to the fact that there was a guy in it who constantly bought everybody free drinks.

Scrooge held criminals in no higher esteem than the rest of us do, but he could not afford to play favorites. The ex-miser assumed that any act of kindness was a point in the proper column, regardless of who the kindness aided, or whether they deserved it. Maybe this was incorrect, but the spirits hadn't left behind a rulebook; if they ever came back (and Scrooge sometimes hoped that they would), he could ask them. Until then, however, he had to play it safe: charity for all. From that day to this, Scrooge had not finished one evening's meal at The Ball and Chain without furnishing everyone's drinks, or meals, or both.

But this evening was different. He tipped well, as usual, but when the bill was presented, no free drinks were announced.

"What are you waiting for, Warden?" Scrooge said to the man behind the bar, who was also the owner. "My change, if you please."

The owner gave Scrooge a puzzled smile. "Aren't you...I just assumed..."

"Not tonight," Scrooge said, firmly. Fred's words had found their mark.

The Warden glanced around, then spoke to Scrooge in low tones. "Pardon me for saying so, sir, but I don't think that's a very good idea. It's meeting night for The Full-Loads, y'see. They'll be wanting their free drink."

The Full-Loads was the name of a local wheelbarrow gang. They terrorized the neighborhood, partying, getting into fights, moving stuff around randomly. They'd scoop up passerby and refuse to let them out unless they paid a ransom. Up until now, Scrooge had been safe, thanks to his nightly generosity.

"It'd be a terrible shame if they 'took you for a ride,'" the Warden said. "A terrible shame." The Warden drew his finger across his throat, suggesting that such a ride might be Scrooge's last, but the ex-miser would not budge.

"You know how it is, Warden," Scrooge said. "Money's always tight around the holidays...It will do everyone good to skip an evening—it will make tomorrow's drink that much more appreciated."

Directly to Scrooge's left, a man resting his face on the bar—a habitual drinker by the name of Sozzle—took loud exception.

"No free drink tonight?" Sozzle cried, raising his head in unsteady indignation. "It's Christmas Eve, Mr. Scrooge! Think of your fellow man! What would Jesus have done?"

Sozzle's mate Sot awoke, and commenced a similar barrage from Scrooge's other side. "I'll tell you what He would've done," Sot said defiantly, "He would've turned the water into wine! Or beer! Or maybe even hard stuff!"

"Some people shouldn't be allowed to read the Bible," Scrooge grumbled, but Sot continued.

"This season is consecrated for the purpose of giving gifts," Sot said. "This is the one time of the year where one can look at his fellows not as competitors or impediments, but as friends."

"Well said, friend," Scrooge replied, leaning heavily on the last word. "While I have given you innumerable free drinks and meals, friend, I'd like to know: what gift have you ever given me?"

Looking down his scarred nose at Scrooge, Sot sniffed, "I never pick your pocket on Sundays. The other days, sure. But Sundays? Never."

Scrooge's face colored. "I wondered—you rascal—"

"No need to thank me," Sot said. "That's simply out of the goodness of me heart."

The rest of the patrons had developed an interest in the discussion, and had gathered behind Scrooge.

"He's got a point," someone said. "He could've robbed you blind."

"*I* would've," another person added. "If I'd only known Sundays were free..."

"Be quiet!" Scrooge demanded. "I weary of your twisted jailbird's logic!"

"Twisted?" "Jailbird?" "Logic?" Whispers circumnavigated the room. As Scrooge received his change, grumbles were building.

"I told you he was no good."

"Once a miser, allus a miser!"

"I'll use his guts for a Christmas stocking!"

Scrooge heard all this, and it made him even more resolved not to break down. After all the kindness he'd shown, this is what everyone thought of him? The old man turned, as to make for the door, but no one moved. He pulled out his miniature shovel and dug gently at the patrons massed between himself and the exit. The crowd of ruffians only wedged in tighter. Someone named Dogmeat wrenched the shovel away from him with a practiced swipe.

"Hallo, you seem to have taken my..." Scrooge went quiet, as Dogmeat snapped the shovel in two, then gave a menacing growl.

Beads of perspiration gathered at various points on Scrooge's person. He turned, and found himself face-to-sternum with the chieftain of the Full-Loads, a pocked and lumpy gentleman everyone called "Axle."

Axle pushed his way to the bar next to Scrooge, and bellowed out an order. "Warden, I'd like my free drink now. Put it on this gentleman's account."

"Yeah!" someone else shouted. "Me, too!" another added.

The Warden looked at Scrooge. "How about it?" he asked.

Now, Scrooge hadn't always been a perfect man, but he was always a brave one—after all, it had taken three full spirits, plus the ghost of his best friend, just to get him to quit being a git. He was equally feisty now. "I don't think so, Warden," Scrooge said. "What you're doing isn't charity. It's extortion."

The Warden saw the malign effect Scrooge's legalistic term had on the crowd, some of whom had spent considerable time in the stripy hole for that very offense. He saw a few removing the prison-themed "flair" from the walls, for use as weapons. Though the Warden placed no particular value on the hide of Ebenezer Scrooge, he had an establishment to protect, and could not afford the inevitable collateral damage. "If it's all the same to you, Mr. Scrooge, I suggest you leave," the Warden said. "I don't want any trouble, especially not on Christmas Eve."

"This is preposterous!" Scrooge said. "I've bought food and drink for everyone in this wretched house!"

"But what have you done for us lately?" Axle snarled, to general approval.

"He's a fraud!" one ruffian said. "I say we throw him out!"

"But take his money first!" another added, slapping a well-used cosh against his palm.

Another whipped out his knife. "I'll make a belt out of his esophagus! A liver makes an excellent cravat!"

Axle turned to Mr. Knife. "Dude, *please*. I just ate."

"Sorry, Axle," Mr. Knife said. "I was just, you know, riffing."

"Well, it's gross. And where did you even learn a word like 'esophagus' anyway? You know what the mid-Victorian school system is like." Axle turned away, then turned back. "You always take it too far, you know? *God!*"

This internecine strife brought the proceedings down a fraction; looking back, it probably saved Scrooge's life. Still, Scrooge's person was far from secure: he was surrounded by inebriated ex-cons, people on the lam from the law, and punks with souped-up wheelbarrows and nothing to lose. As such, he felt it best to attempt another exit quickly, and with as little fanfare as possible.

Scrooge pushed his way through the crowd, which pushed back, hurling curses and spitting. At the door, a particularly large Full-Load blocked his way. This was Sparky, a Full-Load so untouched by civilization that his 'barrow didn't even have a front wheel. He just pushed it, scarring the ground, throwing sparks as he went. People had lost toes, dear reader, and those were the lucky ones!

"Where d'ya think you're goin'?" Sparky said, leering through rotting teeth.

Show no fear, Scrooge thought. They can smell fear. Unfortunately, they could also smell urine, which was collecting in a puddle at Scrooge's feet. "Please don't kill me," he mewled.

"Mebbe I will, and mebbe not," the hulk said. "Ya gotta pay the toll first."

"Oh?" Scrooge asked, his voice quivering. "How much?"

"I dunno—I can't count."

Sparky's horny, vise-like palm closed over the old man's collar. Scrooge's attempts to struggle free were no more than the twisting of a pennant in an ill wind. As the crowd shouted its savage encouragement, the brutal man-mountain roughly turned our hero upside down; then grasping Scrooge by the ankles, began to shake. Coins came tumbling out of Scrooge's pockets, and the crowd scrambled to retrieve them like chickens hard after seed.

The crowd's levity was infectious, and Sparky naturally caught it; when he was laughing too hard to continue his work, he dumped the dazed Scrooge onto the mud-streaked tavern floor. As Scrooge attempted to collect himself, someone reached down and stole the old man's spectacles. This was the signal to begin a spirited performance of "monkey in the middle," with Scrooge cast as the unfortunate banana-grabber.

"Hey! Stop fooling about, now! Those are mine!...All right,

fine, I don't even want th—GIMME!"

It would've lasted longer, had it not been so easy; even society's dregs appreciate a challenge. Truthfully, once they were in possession of Scrooge's liquid assets, the old man ceased to interest any of them, and they went back to plotting various dark enterprises designed to take advantage of people's holiday goodwill.

"Here, Scroogie," one said, waving the eyeglasses. He opened the door, then tossed them outside. "Fetch!"

Scrooge was not even trusted to provide sufficient propulsion for his exit. Sparky's foot on Scrooge's backside ejected him with such force that he was plunged head and shoulders into a snowbank. After extricating himself, the old man spent a cold ten minutes looking for his glasses, as London's rapists, thieves, and murderers pointed and jeered at him through the tavern window.

"Nothing like this ever happened to me when I was a miser," Scrooge griped. "Only the good are so mistreated in this world!" His conscience burned at the injustice. "Just you wait!" he spat quietly at the warm shadows capering inside. "After I die, I'm going to haunt the s—t out of all of you!"

Seeing that Scrooge was saying something to them, the criminals laughed harder, and pounded on the glass until the Warden feared that it might give way. Then they pulled faces at the old man, and oh!—one showed Scrooge his b-m.

Sparky's rough treatment had not helped Scrooge's knee, which was now fairly yodeling for attention; and during the hunt for his glasses, Scrooge somehow succeeded in getting snow down both of his socks. This discomfort was not entirely bad, in that it (as small discomforts sometimes do) focused Scrooge's mind and stimulated an idea.

"Whoop! Hallo!" Scrooge clapped his hands and laughed aloud at the thought of his sparkling new plan. "They'll be f—g sorry they ever messed with 'The Scrooge'!"

Once he'd found his spectacles, the ex-miser walked—ever so casually, now—around the corner, to where all the Full-Load gang's wheelbarrows were propped up against the wall. Checking to see that nobody was watching, he took out his house key. Then, deliberately and with great relish, he scraped it against the garish custom paint-jobs of the 'barrows, marring them severely. On the last, Scrooge even wrote a profanity—then he ran for all he was worth!

The thick atmosphere, and his age, and his lack of a shovel, slowed Scrooge to a crawl; fortunately, everyone inside the bar was busy spending the money they'd liberated from his pockets. After two blocks of giddy flight, he looked behind and saw no one, so he slowed to a normal pace. Scrooge felt invigorated, like a child again. "Whoop!" he said to no one in particular. It echoed off the streets, and shook the snowy trees, and caused people to frown out of parlors that looked warm and inviting. "Merry Christmas, Full-Loads! I've got your present right here!" Scrooge clutched his organ of generation through his pants, and shook it. This was a childish act, there's no denying it. Yet sometimes it is good to be childish, and what time could be better for it than Christmas?

Unfortunately, Scrooge's braggadocio faded as quickly as it had come, and in its place a full measure of bully-dread set in. "What the f—k did I just do?" Scrooge mumbled, walking faster. "A tavern full of ruffians—they're going to beat the s—t out of me." Poor impulse control, a moment of elation, and then pants-pooping fear; yes, dear reader, it was exactly like being a child again.

Now, it may have been the dankness of the atmosphere, or the continuing snow (the flakes were still falling, but more slowly now, as the temperature dropped). It might have been his cracked and filthy glasses, or a trick of his memory, or hallucinations brought on by extremely cold feet. Whatever the cause, when Scrooge arrived at his door, the knocker was not a normal knocker. It was the spitting image of his old partner, Jacob Marley.

Scrooge spied the change from several houses away. "Oh, *give me a break!*" Mounting his steps, the old man looked skyward, assuming that was the right direction to address the spirits. "Not tonight, okay? I'm tired, and there's slush in my shoes."

As if on cue, the papier-mache face dropped to his doorstep

with a clunk. "Damn kids," Scrooge grumbled, embarrassed at his credulity. He kicked the crude mask off his doorstep into the street, and went inside.

THANKS TO the mixture of gelid mud and horse-excrement in which he had been drenched by Tiny Tim's omnibus, Fred trudged home from his Uncle's counting house bone-cold and powerfully rank. After a while, his nose became insensible to it; but Fred knew he stank by the way all the shoppers crossed the street to get out of range. But it was after he arrived at home that his discomfort really began.

As I have said, Fred's wife had never liked Scrooge. At first she refused to believe that the old miser had actually changed. Then, when it was clear that Scrooge's coffers had well and truly been blasted open by fear and remorse, she became determined to get their share of the booty.

Scrooge saw this, and forbore it as best he could. The old man politely declined the shady business deals, real estate scams, and chain-letter schemes she constantly dangled (to say nothing of the sexual favors), while at the same time providing funds for any legitimate need that arose. As long as Scrooge was alive, Fred and his wife need not worry about the wolf at the door.

Unfortunately, Scrooge's decency had only stoked Mrs. Fred's ravenous greed. If Scrooge had refused to help them at all, perhaps Mrs. Fred would've given up, moving on to her other dreams, such as becoming best friends with the Queen. But every little kindness they received reminded Mrs. Fred of the larger things they did not get; her resentment was now of sufficient heat and pressure to run Mr. Fulton's celebrated train. This anger was counterbalanced, and only just, by her fevered fantasies of what she could do with all that Scroogian lucre. These two thoughts became so inflated in her mind that there wasn't room for anything else, certainly not Christmas spirit.

The harridan met her husband at the threshold. "Well?" she demanded.

"Well, what?" Fred said.

"Did the old coot give you anything?" she barked. "You smell like horses—t."

Fred was in no mood. "Perhaps you could let me change clothes before..."

"I should've known! You didn't get a penny!" Mrs. Fred said angrily, cracking him on the head. (Mrs. Fred wore a thimble on her thumb for just this purpose, which she had nicknamed "The Persuader.")

"Ow! F—g h—l!" Fred said, feeling his head, then checking his fingertips for blood.

"Serves you right," a chambermaid offered.

"What's all that lot?" Fred pointed at the stack of boxes the chambermaid was carrying.

"New dresses," Mrs. Fred said defiantly. "Got a problem with that?"

As yet another means of encouraging Fred to french-press more money out of his Uncle, his wife had begun systemically increasing their standard of living. First, she had upgraded her wardrobe—my God! no Sultana or courtesan had anything on Mrs. Fred. "Marie Antoinette had the right idea," she was fond of saying to her husband, "but she just didn't go far enough."

This was followed by the hiring of an army of servants, each of whom more outlandish and unnecessary than the last. Though Mrs. Fred hadn't a scrap of civic spirit, her efforts in this area had made a measureable decrease in the unemployment rate of the district. Charity often works like that, dear reader, and its good shouldn't be discounted a jot for it. It's a rare donation that isn't made for selfish reasons, or to spite someone, or to demonstrate one's place atop the heap—but I digress.

"So did you get some more money, or not?" Mrs. Fred said, ready to dislodge it with another whack.

Fred scrambled away, covering his head. "I think you broke through to my brain!"

Mrs. Fred stopped; a dead husband was no good to her, not yet.

"I'm sorry to have to thump you in front of the help."

"It's all right," Fred said. "They hate me anyway." And they did; Fred had retaliated against his wife's extravagance by "paying" the servants with banknotes he drew himself.

"We hate you, too!" chorused his wife's sisters, *and* that wretched demi-gigolo Topper, who was determined to sleep with all of them even though they thought he was a creep. All of them had moved in, after the money had begun to flow.

"Oh, go home!" Fred said, dumping out the contents of his pockets, and coloring in the thermometer. "I'm quite close..." Fred said. His loins suddenly kindled. "Might you give me a little something...on account?"

Mrs. Fred grabbed his roaming hand and twisted it painfully. "No way, buster. You know the rules."

Fred's pain turned to anger. "Listen, you! I'm your husband, and this is my house, and if you don't start showing me the proper respect, I'll..."

Mrs. Fred turned, all buttons and bows, her Medusa-like locks flouncing. "You'll what?"

"I'll—I'll—!" The fact is he would do nothing; Fred's wife had convinced her rather sheltered husband that she had invented the physical act of love, and was the only one of her gender who knew how to pull it off. So Fred backed down. "I'll—I'll thank you to remember that it's Christmas Eve!"

The mention of the holiday—another one, and here she was, not yet dining at Buckingham Palace—set Mrs. Fred into a fresh rage. "Bah, humbug!" she hollered, working her way about the room, clambering over servants and relatives, destroying expensive, hard-to-replace items at random. "I hate all my stuff!"

Fred watched this with familiar feelings of revulsion and horror. As with other great natural engines of destruction, flight was the only alternative. Unfortunately the army of hangers-on had turned their once-comfortable home into a standing-room-only affair. Still, his stink was a powerful wedge, and Fred was able to push through the crowd halfway to the water closet.

"Don't you dare run away from me," Mrs. Fred yelled. "I sent you over there to get real money out of that stale old freak, and you come back with nothing!"

"Well," Fred said, "it was impossible. He was occupied."

"Giving money away! To other people!" Mrs. Fred saw every act of charity as theft from her pocket.

"But dear, those people are poor," Fred said. "They need it so much more than we do."

"But we're his flesh and blood!"

"Yeah!" bleated a maid sprawled across a nearby divan. She was having her nails done by another maid (who was receiving a pedicure).

"No, you're not!" Fred said. "By the way, that divan is new, isn't it?"

"And what if it is?" Mrs. Fred spat. "What's wrong with my wanting to have nice things? Don't I deserve it? My friend Vicky gets to have nice things and her husband isn't beastly to her!"

Fred grabbed his beard and pulled it in frustration. "First of all, she's not your friend—"

"She is too my friend!"

"No, she's not! She's the Queen, and you're a nutter!"

The room went utterly silent; Fred had said the unsayable.

"O-ho! Get ready, Mr. Bruised-Brain!" Eyes blazing, Mrs. Fred had gathered her skirts and was set to rush across the room to dispense some Victorian justice when a distinguished-looking man appeared in the doorway to the dining room. "Dinner is served."

"Thank God," Fred said. "I'm starving!" He walked full of purpose towards the waiting food, until he was stopped by his bride.

"Uh-uh," she said, stretching herself across the doorway.

"What do you mean, 'Uh-uh'?" Fred said, pushing at her slightly, and enjoying the physical contact.

"I mean, 'Uh-uh,'" Mrs. Fred said. "You're not eating. Not until you go back and get more money from your Uncle. Some real money this time. The kind that folds."

"This is ridiculous! I won't be bossed around in my own house!

Let me through!" Fred gave another push, harder this time, but his wife refused to move. She simply shook her head "no."

A beefy woman got up from the table and shambled over. "Is he bothering you, ma'am?" she rumbled.

Fred was incensed. "Who is that?" he said, pointing. "Who are you?"

"I'm the new governess," the woman said, daring him to do something about it. Other servants, his wife's private army, got up from the dining room table and massed behind her. Fred calculated his odds. He was bigger and stronger than most of them, but there were loads—where did she find them all? Each one clutched a utensil, and wore a hard expression; knowing upon which side their bread was buttered, they relished the prospect of battle.

Fred gave up. "Fine!" he glowered. "I'll go back!" As yet another servant closed the door behind him he shouted, "*A governess? We don't even have children!*"

FRED PULLED his beard and twirled his mustachios, a nervous habit. Scrooge's nephew had reacted to the sudden onset of prosperity in the time-honored fashion, by cultivating a luxurious set of facial hair. His beard and moustachios were so profuse and poky that they called to mind nothing so much as a cat's whiskers. And indeed they performed the same purpose, to prevent Fred's head from getting stuck in holes. A useful thing that, as Fred was tirelessly poking into every tiny facet of Scrooge's affairs, hoping to tease out any profit hidden within.

After his conversation with Scrooge earlier that day, Fred knew he had to come up with a plan. Simply asking wouldn't work. As I have said, Scrooge knew of Fred's wife's designs upon his fortune, and refused—out of principle as well as personal dislike—not to indulge her.

"D—n it," Fred said aloud. It was appreciably colder, and this, plus the closing of most of the stores, meant that the streets were deserted. "You know where there's no bloody snow? *Italy*, that's where!" He kicked a snowdrift in frustration—then found it hid a pile of broken bricks.

Fred's yell woke up some dogs, which in turn caused a few disapproving faces to appear. "Get inside, you drunk!" It only took him two fingers for Fred to respond.

Fred trudged along, limping badly and cursing his lot. The only people who went out on Christmas Eve were people that...had to work. Fred's gorge rose at the thought of it, and he was sick a little, in his mouth.

"This is the most horrible Christmas Eve imaginable! What did I ever do to deserve this?" How Fred longed to be on the other side of every lighted window he passed, warm and content in front of the crackling hearth. How he longed to kick his wife and her bloodsucking staff in some vital, sensitive portion of their anatomies! If only some spirits would visit him this night, and tell him it was okay to do just that!

"What I need," Fred mumbled to no one in particular, "are some spirits of my own." What Man needs, the Creator provides—though it must be said, not always in the expected form; and just as Fred spoke these words, he passed The Ball and Chain. With an unpleasant errand ahead, and nothing but snow and cold wind between himself and the completion of that task, Fred decided to pop in for a drink. A little Christmas drink—what could it hurt?

Fred found a space at the bar between Sozzle and Sot, and set to work. One drink led to two, as it often does; then, three and four. The spirits warmed his brain, and set it to working. By the sixth drink, Fred had birthed an idea on how to finagle his Uncle that he thought was foolproof. Simple, direct, even seasonally appropriate—splendid, if he did say it himself!

The Warden came, bottle in hand. "'Nother?"

"Nah," Fred said thickly. "How much you want for the chains? Up there, on the wall."

"Sorry," the Warden said, scratching his ample belly. A steady stream of freaks came in asking about the "flair." He'd loaned the whips and handcuffs out once, and they'd come back all sticky. "Those are my mum's chains from Bedlam. Not for sale."

"That's okay," Fred said. "I don't wanna buy 'em. I just need to borrow 'em. I wanna play a trick on my Uncle."

"Who's your Uncle?"

"Ebenezer Scrooge," Fred said. "Ex-miser. Now he walks around throwing money at people. Except for me, of course, because—"

The Warden cut him off. "You don't have to tell me who Ebenezer Scrooge is. Earlier tonight he nearly caused a riot."

Well, you could've knocked Fred over with a feather, dear reader. Perhaps his Uncle *wasn't* as boring as a box of dead moths after all.

"Couple of us have a bet," the Warden said. "Do you think he's a flamer?"

Fred shuddered; even inebriated, the thought of his Uncle's sex life was too much to bear. Swallowing back, he said with some difficulty, "So, can I have the chains or not?"

The Warden thought.

Fred pushed the point, and thank goodness he did, for the plot of this book depends on it. "If things break right, he'll c—p his pants." Seeing the Warden wavering, Fred decided to sweeten the deal. "If it works, I'll come and buy everybody a drink."

The Warden got the chains down and handed them to Fred. "Here you go," he said.

"I'll bring 'em back before midnight," Fred said.

"You had better!" the Warden said. "Or else I'll have you back here in a wheelbarrow!"

AFTER ITS BAD beginning, Scrooge's evening had settled down considerably. All was silent; even the neighborhood, which was proudly squalorous, kept its peace on this, the holiest night of the year.

Scrooge had built an unusually large fire, splurging a bit after his cold walk home. Now, as its last embers clinked merrily in the grate, the old man snacked on a plate of gingerbread. Thanks to his change of heart, Scrooge's mania for charity occasionally extended even to himself.

It was amazing how good something as simple as a cookie could taste, after a lifetime of cold gruel. And this treat was doubly tasty, coming as it did from one of the few genuinely needy people to cross Scrooge's path. A few days after his transformation, before the criminals and con men and crooked corporations squeezed out all the decent folk, Scrooge gave some money to an actual widow. She and her non-rented children had moved back to the healthful countryside, where they had relations. Now, every so often, she sent him treats in the mail, out of gratitude. Scrooge thought of her happiness, and savored every bite.

Outside, the wind howled, making Scrooge appreciate his fire all the more—everyone should be safe and fed and warm, he thought, always. All it would take would be for us to decide to make it so; and yet we do not. Why is that? Scrooge dressed for bed, putting on his complimentary clothes; after his story had hit the newspapers, the old man became synonymous with nightshirts and sleeping caps, so a local manufacturer had given him a lifetime supply in exchange for an endorsement.

But even though he was warm, well-fed, and swaddled in swag, Scrooge was not quite content; it is a lamentable fact that worries and cares have a tendency to emerge just before bedtime, and Scrooge was not immune to this. Decapitating his last cookie, Scrooge pondered the events of the evening. It would've been so much simpler just to buy everyone drinks. But by not doing so he had discovered the truth: His charity was not making him loved. Most took without a thought—and thoughtlessness was the best he could hope for! The rest actively despised Scrooge for a fool!

"The spirits made it seem so simple," Scrooge sighed. "Perhaps it is—on their plane. Here wickedness taints everything, even acts of goodness." Scrooge looked at the blue-painted tiles of his fireplace and focused on his favorite, one of Salome. This buxom cartoon was all that the old bachelor had in the way of female companionship, and he did with it what he could.

"I realize Fred squeezes me, down to the last vinegary dreg;

I see Cratchit leveraging my sympathy into more trollops and coconut oil! But what can I do, Salome? What can anyone do?" Scrooge addressed these questions to the tile, his passion rising to its height. "For the sake of my soul, I must give. But how, without simply gilding the world's wickedness and misery?...I wish the spirits would come again tonight, not to tell me to give, but teach me how! Oh! *Oh! OH!*"

Scrooge's passion faded. "If only the world was the way it is in books," he sighed, spent. Perhaps tomorrow he would find the answer. If any day could show him the right kind of kindness, surely it would be Christmas?

Scrooge turned things over in his mind as he drifted off to sleep. Maybe charity does begin at home, as Fred said. But Fred's wife was such a harpy! Helping strangers was so much more appealing, because you didn't know what jerks they *really* were... Still working this puzzle, Scrooge fell into a deep and restful sleep.

As a result, the old man became aware of the noise outside only by small degrees. Someone was rummaging around in the street below...kids, probably. No, it wasn't children, the steps were too heavy; it was a man. Was he drunk? In *this* neighborhood? Scrooge leaned over and stuck tuppence into the pipe by his bed—it snaked down and emptied out onto the sidewalk. Conscience salved, Scrooge decided that whoever it was, they would finish their business and go away...

But they didn't. Scrooge couldn't make out what was happening; it seemed like the man was attempting to open the door. This didn't alarm Scrooge—the door was heavy enough, and the lock secure—but it didn't let him fall back asleep, either. A scrape, a thump, a muffled curse—who was it? And what in blazes were they doing? Scratch, scratch, scratch...Just soft enough to be heard, too regular to be the wind; it was as if a drop of water was hitting Scrooge's forehead at irregular intervals, with each drop's impact nudging him infintesimally further from slumber.

Scrooge lay in bed between sleep and wakefulness for what seemed like an age—then, in a moment, his guts turned to ice!

That was a moan, he knew that sound! And the rattle of a chain! Suddenly bolt upright, Scrooge pulled the covers to his chin. He waited, too frightened to move.

"Just a trick of the mind, that's all," Scrooge said in as firm a voice as he could manage. "Or a nightmare. I know I *believe* I'm awake, but some dreams are like that. Totally understandable on the one-year anniversary..." Speaking the circumstance aloud made him even more frightened, but this was nothing compared to how he felt when he heard another rattle.

"Ebenezer SCROOGE!" a voice called, the wind shifting between words so that the last name sounded louder, like an accusation.

"Oh!" Scrooge cried out. "Go away, spirits! I have done as you wished, why are you tormenting me? I don't want to see you again, I was only kidding!"

"Good, you're home," the voice noted matter-of-factly. Then the voice and the rattling became louder still. "EBENEZER SCROOGE!" the being commanded. "LET ME IN!"

Scrooge's fear dissolved for a moment—Let him in? Can't he walk through walls? They could last year. Scrooge cleared his throat, then addressed the spirit. "My slippers are all the way across the room. Why can't you just glide up here yourself?"

Scrooge heard swearing. Did the spirits swear last year?

"DON'T"—the wind shifted again—"argue!"

Leaving his warm bed unwillingly, Scrooge lit a candle, then padded to the top of the stairs. "Who is it?" he said.

"Jacob Marley's ghost."

"Oh, for God's—Jacob, why do you torment me? Everybody knows I learned my lesson. Don't they have newspapers where you are?"

"Uh..." Then the voice began again: "FOOLISH MORTAL! Do you dare question the wishes of the spirit world?"

"No-ooo," Scrooge equivocated, "but I was really hoping this wouldn't become an annual thing. Also, you sound drunk."

"And *you* sound just like my wife!"

"Since when are you married, you pederast?" Scrooge scratched his gut sleepily. "Listen, Jacob: the party's over. Go find one of your rent-boys and crash on their couch—"

Downstairs on the stoop, Fred gave his chains an angry rattle. After a mournful moan, however, he went blank. What the hell do ghosts say? "Ebenezer Scrooge, you have more yet to learn..."

"Like what? Send me a letter."

"Cheeky b—d!" Fred said. "I'll tell you when you let me in!"

Marley was just as headstrong as ever, Scrooge thought; there was never a tougher man of business, nor a more difficult person to get rid of. For God's sake, the man had been dead for years, and here he was, still showing up at all hours!

"You better have a bottle of champagne, that's all I can say." Reluctantly, Scrooge padded down the stairs. It was freezing in the stairway. "I've given away a ton of money, Jacob," Scrooge said through the door. "If there was more to it than that, really, I think it's got to be on you guys."

"Do not argue!" Fred yelled, teeth chattering in the cold. "St-t-t-tubborn sh-sh—t!"

Hand on the lock, Scrooge paused. "I distinctly remember you walking through walls."

Fred was losing feeling in his extremities. "For God's sake, let me in! It's bloody freezing!"

"OI! SHADDUP!" somebody yelled. Several neighborhood dogs began to bark.

In the name of peace and quiet, Scrooge opened the door. There standing before him was his old partner Jacob Marley. Well, sort of—Marley was taller than he remembered him, and thinner, and had more hair on his head than Scrooge remembered, too. Since when did Marley have a moustache? But Scrooge was an old man, with vision to match. And who else would be visiting him on this day, and this hour? It had to be Marley.

"Thank Christ!" Fred said, shuffling inside. "Take your sweet time, don't you?"

"Jacob, I ask again: why do you torment me?" Scrooge said, after he'd closed the door and locked it. "Can we make this brief? I've had a busy day—giving money to the needy, don't you know."

Fred hurried past and up the stairs. "I'll explain everything," he said, his chains jingling merrily as he walked. "Tell me you haven't let the fire go out. I can't feel my thighs."

Five minutes later, Scrooge and the spirit were sitting in front of a fire Scrooge had coaxed back to life. Fred was in Scrooge's favorite armchair, and the ersatz spirit had a hot toddy in his hand.

"Jacob, I thought you were insensible to heat and cold," Scrooge said rather snottily. Nobody sat in his favorite chair.

"Yes, well," Fred said between slurps, "when you've lived where I have for the last eight years, you get used to a certain level of warmth."

At the mention of eternal torment, Scrooge broke again; he instantly fell to his knees, and grasped the eerie visitor around the ankles. "Oh, Jacob!" he said. "I've done as you asked—as all the spirits asked! Save me from h—l!" Scrooge looked up, with tears in his eyes. "It was that thing with the wheelbarrows, wasn't it?" he said in a piteous voice. "I'll buy them all new ones, I promise."

"Why does everybody keep mentioning wheelbarrows?" Fred said. "I have no idea what you're talking about."

Scrooge's manner changed instantly. "Thank God! I mean, forget it," Scrooge said, straightening up. "But Jacob, haven't I done as you asked?" The old man tugged at the chains that wound around the ersatz spirit. "These are lighter, are they not?"

"Hey!" Fred said, "I have to return those. Get up off the floor."

"Okay," Scrooge said. This year's Marley seemed much less ominous—almost ridiculous, compared to last year's version. "Hey, spirit," the ex-miser said, "do your jaw thing again."

"What?"

"You know, the trick with your jaw—you untie it, and it falls to the floor," Scrooge said. "I loved that."

Scrooge hadn't been shy about revealing the details of his Christmas visit from the spirits, but there were certain aspects

Fred couldn't approximate. For someone tipsy and in a hurry, the con-man had done quite a good job. In addition to wrapping himself in light chain, Fred had put some cold porridge in his hair, and pulled it into a Satanic-looking mess before letting it dry. Then he wrapped a handkerchief around his jaws—which, obviously, did not detach.

"NO!" Fred boomed, spilling his drink. "I did not come all this way to perform parlor tricks, Ebenezer Scrooge! I must deliver a further message regarding your immortal soul."

"Do me a favor, and blot the chair first," Scrooge said. "You got toddy on it."

"Oh. Sorry." He untied his jaws, and blotted the liquor with the cloth. "Anyway, about your immortal soul—"

"I'm all ears," Scrooge said.

"What?"

"It means 'I'm listening,'" Scrooge said. Had Marley's ghost gotten stupider? Was that possible? Certainly he was a lot less terrifying than Scrooge remembered, though the old man couldn't put his finger on why. Maybe it was the fact that he had brought a page of notes, which he referred to as he spoke.

"Scrooge," Fred said, scanning the crumpled sheet in his hand, "you have misunderstood the visit from the spirits. You have been generous, it is true, and while that is part of our message, there is another part. It is not enough to give—you must give wisely!"

"Funny thing," Scrooge said, already wishing he were asleep, "I was just talking to my nephew Fred about that this afternoon."

"A wise man, that Fred."

"You know of him? In your world?"

"Most certainly," Fred said. "He is known as a noble, wise, and kind man. One of the sages of the Ages. In fact, in the opinion of all of us, you could do a lot worse than giving all your money to him."

Scrooge noticed that Marley wasn't as translucent this year. "You guys know about his wife, right?"

"Oh...sure..." Fred wasn't used to thinking on his feet, and the extra-ominous Marley voice was hurting his throat. He really wished he'd hired an actor. "She seems like a worthy woman."

"Not from down here, she doesn't," Scrooge snorted. "To us, she seems like a two-ton, nickel-plated, steam-powered b—h."

"Remember where I live, mortal," Fred said, backpedaling. "There are comparatively few females...down there."

"Well, make room for one more," Scrooge said.

"Look," Fred said impatiently, "I didn't schlep all the way here wrapped in bondage gear to argue with you about whether Fred's wife is a b—h or not. This is about saving your immortal soul. And there is only one way you can do that: give money to Fred."

"I already give him a little," Scrooge said. "I bought him a nice corkscrew for his birthday."

"Oh, well, then!" Fred said sarcastically. He put down his drink, and gave the light chain an annoyed rattle. "Not enough! Not enough! Ebenezer Scrooge, you have a lifetime of wrongs to fix! You must act quickly, and with all your heart! For the sake of your immortal soul, funnel cash to your nephew *tout suite!*"

"All of it?" Scrooge asked, hoping the answer was no. He liked being Sir Gives-a-lot. For one thing, women occasionally kissed him.

"Ideally, yes," Fred said. "Or you can leave it to him after you're dead. For now, just give him a big old chunk. And more whenever he asks for it." Fred rattled his chains. "Or else you'll end up like me-e-e!" Fred tried to give a super-bloodcurdling moan, but his booze-roughened voice gave out. It was time for him to go. Coughing, he moved towards the door.

Scrooge pounded him on the back. "Jacob, were you always so...solid?"

"Yes," Fred croaked. "I just chose to be different this year, is that all right with you?"

"Sure, sure. But aren't you going to fly out the window? What's next, using public transportation?"

"Enough prattling, mortal! Do not bother me with trifling questions about things you cannot understand—just remember what I've said to you tonight!"

"That I should stop throwing money at everybody who asks,

and give it to Fred instead?"

"Yes!" Fred turned to go. "Charity begins at home."

Scrooge grabbed the spirit's jacket, which seemed strangely sweaty. "What about Tiny Tim?"

"What about him?" Fred said.

"Surely I should still give money to him," Scrooge said. "Surely he—"

"No!" Fred said quickly. "That kid's a stone thug! Trust us, we know all, see all." Fred started down the stairs.

"But he's crippled…"

"Maybe he's faking," Fred shouted behind him. "Anyway, so what? Crippled people can be jerks, too."

Scrooge thought of something. "Jacob!" he cried from the top of the stairs. "Wait!"

Fred tripped on his chains and fell heavily against the door. "What, what, WHAT?"

"Is this the only visit tonight?" Scrooge asked. "Or will there be more spirits, as there were last time?"

"No, this is it." Fred opened the door and plunged out. "Farewell, Unc…" he caught himself. "…Ebenezer Scrooge!"

The blast of wind from the open door blew out Scrooge's candle. The old man took this as his cue to go back to bed.

"Only one this year," Scrooge said, pulling the covers to his chin, and nestling back in. "At least that's an improvement."

IN HIS HASTE to leave, Fred opened Scrooge's door right into Tiny Tim's nasty, malevolent manservant. "Watch it!" growled the slight-but-menacing Crippen. He was checking the "**FREE MONEY! TAKE SOME**" bucket Scrooge kept on his front steps.

"Already checked it," Fred said. He had always loathed Crippen.

The feeling was mutual. "It's Christmas Eve, not Halloween," Crippen said, looking at Fred's costume.

Fred made a face. "Did the zoo let you out for the holiday?"

"Oh, good one." Both men were now crammed in Scrooge's

doorway, and neither would back down or step aside. Fred put his left fist behind him, and began wrapping the light chain around it. Simultaneously, Crippen was sneaking his hand into the pocket of his overcoat, feeling for his trusty sand-filled sock. But before battle could commence, Tiny Tim stuck his head out of the pimped-out omnibus parked nearby. Four teams of horses idled in front of it—it was a hot-rod, faster than anything the cops had. "Anything in the bucket?" the hardboiled runt asked.

"No, 'Master T,'" Crippen said.

"Well, then, let's move on," Tim said, in a high yet commanding voice. He looked at Fred. "What are you doing here, d—knose?"

Crippen's beating would have to wait. "The same thing you are. You'll be dismayed to know that I've derailed your little gravy train. Permanently!"

"Bah!" Crippen said, spitting into the snow. "Should I thrash him?" he asked Tim.

Fred laughed, but there was no jolliness in it. "You? Thrash me?" For all his talk, Crippen was incredibly weak—they all were, thanks to rampant malnutrition and lungs filled with coal dust—but Crippen was particularly so. He looked like something you might find coiled at the bottom of a drain, only less cuddly.

"Enjoy the high life while you still can, w—kers," Fred said triumphantly. "Uncle's just had a visit from a new spirit. Can you guess what that new spirit said?" He looked at Crippen. "I'm asking Tim. I know you couldn't guess."

"That I'm going to kill you?" Crippen growled, fingering his sand-filled sock. (At least I think it was his sand-filled sock.)

Before Tim could give an answer, a feminine hand emerged from the inside of the omnibus and tousled his young locks. "Come back inside, Master T! Don't bother with those nasty men!"

"B—h!" Tim slapped blindly. "I'm working!"

All of it was just too sordid for Fred. "The spirit said to cut you off, Tim. Not another cent. And I think Scrooge believed him."

"You b—d," Tim piped, adding to the truly shameful number of swears in this book.

Fred began to walk away. "Someday you'll realize that the world is run on brains, not brawn," he told them. "Now, if you'll excuse me, I have a little celebration to attend."

Tim and Crippen watched Fred walk away. "Should I kill 'im *now*, boss?"

"No," Tim said, allowing his spoon-chested henchman to have his fantasies of lethality. "As much as I'd love that, we haven't bought enough policemen in this district, and you're too valuable to let you go to prison."

"Thanks, boss."

"It's nothing personal. HEY!"—Tim rounded on a hottie— "would you stop pinching my b—m?" Then he disappeared into the holly-bedecked booty caravan.

Ignoring the giggles, Crippen mounted the driver's perch. They had gone less than a block when Tim stuck his head out again. "I've just had an excellent idea. The Majestic Theater, Crippen, as fast as these nags can take us!"

As they passed Fred, Tim threw an empty champagne bottle at him. It missed Fred's noggin by inches.

"Missed!" Fred taunted. "Get ready for the workhouse, you scum!" He heaved a snowball with a large rock in its middle.

It cracked a window, but the conveyance drove on. Time was of the essence, and Tim's dark purposes would not wait.

"No, I have never heard of The Doors," Scrooge said.

STAVE THREE.

———•———

A MEMORABLE PERFORMANCE.

TINY TIM WAS NOT kind, or cheerful, or thoughtful, or concerned with others more than himself. He wasn't even (and this is strange to hear, I know) a cripple. What Tim was, dear reader, was a master of deceit, a perfect monster really, and the true facts of his existence are enough to make anyone ponder what they think they know about their fellows. Here was a man born to be a politician, and I don't think I need to say any more than that.

Timothy Cratchit came into the world poor, but that did not decide anything; the majority of the world is similarly shackled, and yet most struggle within the boundaries of morality. But Tiny Tim was different: Like many of history's greatest criminals, he had been cursed with the gift to see his situation too clearly at too tender an age. He saw his father was an overgrown child, unequal to the task of raising his brood; his mother, on the other hand, was a sphinx of passivity, ignoring anything she did not wish to see; and about his siblings, the less said, the better!

Put simply, there was not enough to go around; and as the youngest, Tim needed the good opinion of others to survive. What else could he do but inflate their affections? What else could he do but play upon their sympathy? In every outward aspect Tim strove to be kind, cheerful, sensitive, decent. And to give everyone's heartstrings that final pluck, at the age of three Tim decided to become crippled, too.

Nobody noticed that his crutch shifted arms, or that he was somehow strong enough to capture an escaped alligator, which subsequently became his own lethal pet. One time, Tim used the iron frame supposedly supplementing his withered limbs to maim a child thrice his size. (The boy's crime? Beating Tim at marbles.) Tim said it was an accident, and who could doubt a poor little crippled boy?

His family offered Tim their meals; Tim ate them. His father carried him to and from school on his shoulders; Tim enjoyed the ride. Whenever he thought someone might be catching on, or sensed a small decrease of sympathy, Tim was ready with a "relapse"—though what disease he had was never clear. The other Cratchits weren't the type to ask, or think to ask, or think.

In this way, he secured his boyhood, and stood at the head of his family. Had he not been committed to the easy way, Tiny Tim might've been a truly remarkable man, worthy in every respect. But Tim was determined to rise in the world, whatever it took. He waited for his opportunity in hiding, like a cunning beast of prey.

Ebenezer Scrooge was that opportunity. Tim did not believe in spirits—his Universe was uncaring and cruel, and did not contain ethereal beings that dispensed moral lessons. What Tim did believe in was money. And so, along with everyone else, he set about getting as much of that sweet Scroogian bullion as possible.

God, how easy it was! The old man was so sentimental, and there was always something more to buy for "poor little Tim"; Scrooge's outlay for new crutches alone was more than enough for Tim to buy the omnibus.

But it was another gift from Scrooge that allowed Tim to truly prosper: fame. As I have said, Scrooge's visitation was widely known, and no one came off better in those accounts than the humble, pathetic, good-hearted urchin Tiny Tim (it sickens me just to write it!). Scrooge was visited December 24th; by February 1st, every schoolchild in London knew and admired Tim. This made stealing their clothes a piece of cake.

Here's how it went down: Crippen would drive the omnibus to one of London's posh neighborhoods, and park it outside a particularly spiffy-looking school. As classes let out, the children would immediately see the sign on the side of the 'bus:

"Meet 'Tiny Tim'!

Urchin to the Stars! England's Favorite Cripple!

INQUIRE WITHIN!"

Naturally, students would stream into the omnibus, where Tim sat in the back, surrounded by sweets and toys. When the bus was filled,

Tim would slip upstairs to the roof, locking the door behind him. Most of the time, the students wouldn't even notice, enjoying the carnival-like atmosphere. "Ooh, Sybil! Cholmondeley! We're moving!"

Crippen would drive the omnibus to a deserted region far from the school; then the captives (who were still busy playing, eating sweets and chatting), would be given a ultimatum: if they wished to see their families ever again, they had to strip off their clothes and leave them in the bins beneath each seat. There was always some crying, and Crippen occasionally had to twist an ear or two ("See what happens when you try to be a hero?") but most complied without comment. After they'd done so, they were released to wander back home in their underwear.

In this way, Tim quickly generated a fortune in the second-hand clothes trade. No one believed the stories of his victims, such was the goodwill generated by the original tale. And what kid wanted everyone to know that he'd been duped by a cripple? As usual, Tiny Tim had worked out all the angles.

It was a good living—a great one, in fact—but there were only so many upper-class children to fleece; much to Tim's chagrin, the rich did not reproduce as fast as the poor. So Tim had to branch out into other pursuits, if his criminal empire was going to grow. His first foray into this was the recent purchase of The Majestic Theatre, which Scrooge had unwittingly paid for. (Tim had faked a fall down some stairs "attempting to save a beautiful kitten.")

What Tim planned to do with the theater was unclear as yet. Crippen was encouraging him to torch it for the insurance, preferably with enough people still in it to distract the police. Tim wasn't sure, but he knew what sounded good: every actress' affections, it was said, were available for a fee. And just to give himself maximum range, Tim had assembled a very special troupe, where every actor was more than just a thespian—a pickpocket, perhaps, or a forger, a mountebank, a charlatan, a grifter, a ninja.

To keep salaries low, Tim allowed his troupe to live rent-free at the Majestic. As a result it had become a colorful place, with all sorts of dubious and eccentric types coming and going at all hours. The

Majestic was never silent before three or four in the morning, and Christmas Eve was no exception: theater people follow older Gods, and wilder. Dionysus, the Lizard King, still lived at the Majestic.

So when Tim arrived, everyone was still up. Crippen hastily assembled them all, uncoupling some, pouring black coffee down the throats of others. "Everybody come to the stage!" Crippen yelled, pounding on one door after the other. "Master T's got a job for you!"

Perched upon Crippen's shoulders, Tim addressed the troupe. "Good evening, all. Merry Christmas."

"Merry Christmas," the troupe replied, in anything from a grunt to a giggle depending on their mental state.

"You all know Ebenezer Scrooge, don't you?"

"'Course we do," a girl with mussed make-up said.

"Ex-miser, now everybody's favorite mark," said an older man who stank of pomade. "Nobody's as trusting as a convert."

"Yes, well, there's been some talk—loose talk—that he's going back to his old penny-pinching ways," Tim said. "Naturally, we can't let that happen."

"But what can we do about it?" the girl said.

"Plenty," Tim said. "I've got a plan, but I need your help. Here's what we're going to do..."

BACK IN SCROOGE'S apartment, the old man laid in bed, awake. There was something about Marley's visit that bothered him, something not quite right. But after a half-hour without being able to put his finger on it, Scrooge was finally able to drift away.

Scrooge had been comatose for about an hour when he felt a sharp poke in the foot. Turning over, the ex-miser resolved to avoid the shepherd's pie at The Ball and Chain. The dish always gave him nightmares (and he occasionally found a file in it).

"Get up!" a voice said.

"Ouch!" This time the poke really hurt. Scrooge propped himself upon his elbows, and saw a shadowy figure at the foot of his bed. "Look, go away! Marley said there would be no more ghosts."

Scrooge flopped back down. "One day off a year," he grumbled into his pillow, "That's all I ask..."

Scrooge's ankle was caught in a strong, chilly grip. "Come on," the voice at the end of the bed said. "Everybody's waiting."

The figure began pulling Scrooge out of bed from the bottom.

"Hey!" Scrooge said, now fully awake and perturbed. "Quit it!" He kicked, to no avail; grabbing onto the bedclothes was similarly useless, and Scrooge soon found himself on the floor in a pool of sheets. "All right," Scrooge said, slowly getting to his feet. "Just who the h—l are you? How did you get in downstairs?"

"I'm the Ghost of—" Crippen checked a greasy, crumpled note—"Christmas Past. Locked doors mean nothing to me."

"So Marley was wrong," Scrooge said, relieved somehow. "Ghosts can still go through doors."

"Of course," Crippen said. (He'd smashed the lock with a paving stone.)

"Have you seen Marley? He looks different, doesn't he?" Scrooge went to light a taper.

The figure said in a stern voice, "No candles, please."

"Was Marley wrong about the other ghosts? I'm going to be up all night, aren't I?"

"Marley is crazy," Crippen said. "We all make fun of him. Now, put on some clothes, we're going on a journey."

"But last year—" Scrooge stopped himself; even in the gloom he could see that the ghost was annoyed, and this ghost was nobody you wanted angry. Though small, it was menacing, scorpion-like; and it was swinging a sand-filled sock. As he dressed, Scrooge attempted to chat it up.

"You're new, aren't you?" Scrooge simpered. "I like you much better than the spirit last year. Old, young, million arms, no arms, light coming out of its head—what a freak!"

Crippen was silent. He'd dumped himself into a chair and was studying his fingernails with a look that suggested they'd wronged him somehow, and he was looking forward to giving them the beatdown they so richly deserved. This was Crippen's expression for all occasions. When Scrooge was nearly finished, Crippen got up and left the room without a word.

"So, we're flying again?"

Crippen didn't answer, tromping down the stairs heavily.

"Okay, no problem. Walking's fine." Scrooge followed, pulling on his greatcoat. "Though I must admit I rather liked zipping around without feeling the cold..." They got to the front door. "What happened here?" Scrooge asked, handling the smashed lock which now hung loosely from the side of the splintered door.

Crippen didn't say anything, and continued to walk to the hansom cab parked out front.

"Hey!" Scrooge said. "We can't just leave! My house is completely open—somebody will rob it!"

A figure smelling of pomade opened the door of the cab, and called to Scrooge. "Why not let them take it all—as a Christmas present?" the driver suggested in a plummy, overcheerful voice.

Scrooge disliked him immediately; he was preening and perfumed, which Scrooge found unpleasant in man or ghost. Scrooge cast a glance back at his door, which was now swinging in the winter wind. "Look, this neighborhood is loaded with robbers, squatters, roving drunkards...It's only a matter of time before—"

"Time? What is time to an immortal spirit like me?" the ghost said. His features were jowly, rouged and entirely insipid. "Hurry up and step inside. My feet are freezing."

Scrooge gave up; he knew better than to argue with a spirit.

The instant the door was closed, the cab sprang forward. Scrooge fell against the creature, who certainly felt like a man. None of these spirits made any sense!

"You're not a ghost," Scrooge ventured boldly. "Since when do ghosts wear lilac aftershave?"

"I beg your pardon!" the creature said. "I am the Ghost of Christmas Past!"

"Then who is he?" Scrooge asked, pointing at the driver.

"Also myself. I can take many forms," the Ghost said.

Scrooge leaned out the window, attempting to see if the cab

was driving itself.

"It's no use doing that," the Ghost said. "The moment you take your eyes off me, I transform into him, and vice-versa. Now close the window!"

Scrooge sunk back into his seat, frustrated. "I have to use the bathroom," he lied petulantly.

"Hold it until we arrive. It's not far."

The spirit was true to its word; within seven minutes, the cab stopped. "All ashore that's going ashore!" the spirit said.

Scrooge stepped out of the cab quickly, getting snow up his trouserleg. But he was nonetheless grateful, for the heavy scent of the spirit's hair oil was nauseating in the extreme. He found himself in front of a door—it was the stage door of the Majestic Theater, but there was no way for Scrooge to know that; neither miserdom nor his new career had afforded much time for attending plays. Above the door hung a crude sign which read, "This Way to the Spirit World."

Scrooge paused, feeling for the hundredth time that evening that the spirit world had really gone downhill in the last year, and that he'd rather be home in bed. He was about to express these sentiments in a particularly forceful fashion when the spirit behind him urged him forward.

"Hurry, hurry, we don't have all night."

Scrooge looked behind and saw the figure from his bedroom and the spirit that reeked of aftershave and pomade. Both at once. Standing next to each other. "Wait, there's something fishy—"

The pomaded one gave Scrooge a push through the door, then the other spectre added a gratuitous and very unspectral kick to Scrooge's backside.

The old man was immediately in pitch black. His other senses sharpened, Scrooge could smell paint and freshly sawn wood.

"Hallo?" he called. "Is there anybody here?" There was no answer. "This is different from last year, fellows—that time, nobody just left me...or swore at me...or kicked me..."

Still no answer. Slowly, as he stood there in the darkness and silence, Scrooge's annoyance turned into trepidation. "I'm getting out of here," he said aloud, then began feeling for the doorknob —it must be right here. But try as he might, Scrooge could not find it; it was too dark, and he kept sticking his hand into spider's webs. Then he stepped on something crunchy, and the willies overtook him.

"Help!" he cried out. "Help!"

A door opened, and the chamber was flooded with light. "Calm yourself," a high voice said.

Scrooge could not make out the figure. The light was too much for the old man's eyes. He felt the spirit take his arm.

"Come with me."

The spirit was small—and familiar, somehow. Could it be Tiny Tim? Oh, no! Say it wasn't so—Tim had succumbed to his illness (whatever it was) and had passed on! Then Scrooge looked again: though they could be twins, this was not the Tim he knew

"See these child actors?" asked the spirit. "Without your help, they will not be able to afford cocaine."

and loved. Tiny Tim walked with a crutch, while this child was whole—small, to be sure, but hale and hearty. Also, Tim didn't wear a suit with wide lapels. Or a hat with a leopard band. Or carry a bejeweled pimp's goblet. Or call women "ho."

As the spirit led Scrooge on a circuitous route through the bowels of the theater, Scrooge's brain burned with questions. Perhaps it *was* poor Tim, but in his spirit form, when all our maladies and troubles have been lifted. Could it be Tim's ghost, visiting from the future?

Scrooge shook his arm free. "Tell me, who are you, spirit? For good or ill, I must know—are you...?

"I am the Ghost of Christmas Past."

"You, too? Thank Heaven!" Scrooge said, almost sobbing with emotion. "I thought you were someone I knew, a dear, sweet boy of my acquaintance..." The more Scrooge thought of it, the more laughable it was. This slick character, Tiny Tim? Ridiculous. "Where are we going?" Scrooge asked buoyantly.

They went through a door onto a balcony. "Sit," the spirit commanded.

"Are we going to see a performance?" Scrooge asked.

"Of sorts," the spirit said, in a high voice. It pointed to the stage. "Now, look!"

The stage blazed into light. Then a actor came out from behind the curtain and spoke.

"Ebenezer Scrooge," the man said, "you have disregarded the warnings of the spirits—"

"That's not true!" Scrooge shouted. He turned to the child-sized spirit beside him, who was fingering a large pinky ring. "I swear it's not!"

"Even though you are surrounded by misery and want, your resolve is weakening!" the man continued. "You must keep giving! Unless you want to end up in...*H—L!*" A chorus of wails and moans echoed through the theater, sending a shiver up Scrooge's spine. Then the stage went dark.

There were sounds of people moving things around. Normally

Scrooge would've been unimpressed at the absence of magic—this year's ghosts were really quite lackluster, maybe he should give some money to *them*. But some small residue of awe remained, so Scrooge stayed silent.

The small spirit leaned over. "Whatever Marley told you," he whispered, "don't listen. Don't be a chump—don't suffer eternal torment, just because some idiot misheard God."

Before Scrooge could answer, the stage was lit again. In the middle of it, a boy sat alone, reading a book. Behind him was the backdrop of a circus.

"That's me, spirit!" Scrooge cried aloud. "Poor, friendless, alone, with only my books for company...I don't remember the circus part, though."

"Oh, that's...um," Tim cleared his throat. Damn propmaster was hitting the opium again. "It was a long time ago, and you are old and forgetful."

"Yeah, but I think I would—"

Tim leapt onto his chair. "WRETCHED SINNER!" Tim shouted, his prepubescent voice skirling into the higher registers. "THE SPIRITS KNOW ALL! DO YOU DARE CONTRADICT..."

"Okay, okay," Scrooge said, unconvinced. "Simmer down. Jeez." These ghosts were all so touchy.

Scrooge sat in silence, as groups of children teased and mocked his younger self. Their *coup de grace* came when the boy was forced to eat raw toad guts. As he lay on the stage crying, a young female came out.

"Poor brother," the girl said, kneeling down and stroking his offal-caked cheek.

"Dear Fan," the boy said, voice quaking. "Dear, dear, Fan. Why do they all hate me so?"

"Who cares?" Fan shrugged. "They'd like you if you gave them some money."

"Would they?" the boy said, suddenly hopeful. "Would they really, truly like me?"

Scrooge stood up. "No, they wouldn't!" he yelled, thinking of the ruffians at The Ball and Chain.

Tim tugged on Scrooge's jacket. "They cannot hear you, Scrooge," he said.

It certainly didn't seem like that to Scrooge. Both performers had jumped a mile, and now seemed to be totally thrown by his outburst. "Would they really, truly like me?" the boy said again.

The girl paused, then hollered, "Line!"

"'No, not really...'" a voice whispered from the wings. "'They'd just be...'"

"No, not really," Fan said, picking up the thread. "They'd just be using you. But they wouldn't make you eat raw frog guts."

"Well," the boy said, "I guess that's something,"

With that, the stage went dark. When the lights came up again, Scrooge recognized the players immediately.

"Why, it's old Fezziwig," Scrooge said. "I apprenticed for him. What a kind, generous old fellow he was!"

"You think that? Then you learned nothing from your apprenticeship," Tim said.

"I do not understand, spirit."

Stifling a yawn, the spirit refused to explain. "Keep watching."

"Would you just tell me?" Scrooge asked. "You know what I hate the most about you ethereal beings? You're all so snotty!"

"What do you expect?" Tim said. "We know all and see all."

"Sure, but do you have to be such d—ks about it?" Scrooge's voice grew louder as he warmed to his topic. "Sure, it's easy for you spooks to tell me, 'Give it all away'–what do you need money for? You don't have to eat. You don't have to pay rent. I promise you this," Scrooge said, "one night of going hungry and all you shades would sing a different song indeed."

"Excuse me," one of the actors called up to them, "but we're trying to portray the most poignant moments of your life down here."

"Yeah," another added. "Least you could do is shut up."

"I didn't ask for this," Scrooge said. "Anyway, I'm sure you're all getting Equity rates."

"We'll talk about it later," Tim called down to his employees, anticipating the fight. "Carry on."

The stage had about ten people on it, reenacting the Christmas revels at the Fezziwigs'. They were all dancing and swinging each other around wildly, and bellowing things like, "Jolly good quadrille!" and "You're stepping on my corns!" and "This is the best Christmas ever!" It wasn't exactly as Scrooge remembered it—once again, the backdrop suggested it was taking place at a circus—but after the way the Ghost jumped down his throat the last time, he wasn't about to say anything.

The fiddler was awful, but Fezziwig fairly loaded him down with coin. He did the same to everyone else present at the dance, including their dog.

"Why, he's almost Scroogian in his generosity," Tim whispered to Scrooge.

"More fool him," Scrooge griped. "Probably counterfeit."

"It does not matter," Tim said. "Do you see how happy everyone is, including Fezziwig himself? Do you understand why?"

"Sure," Scrooge said. "And I also get why he always paid such c—p wages."

"There are more important things than business," Tim said. "Love, for example."

The stage had been cleared, and only two actors remained—the young, gangly one meant to be Scrooge, and a young lady.

"You have changed," the woman said to the man. "You never buy me presents anymore."

"It's not I who have changed," the stage-Scrooge said. "It's Fezziwig. He's cut our pay. We will never be able to marry, unless I economize."

From the balcony, Scrooge hooted with glee at his stand-in's defiance. "That's right! You tell 'em, Scrooge!"

The young lady was unconvinced. "I don't think you need to worry yourself on that score," she said, "as I do not wish to marry a cheapskate."

"Sensible girl," Tim said to Scrooge. "Pity you let her get away."

"Have you ever met my nephew Fred's wife?" Scrooge asked.

THERE HAD BEEN a final scene, drawn quite vividly and aimed quite cruelly, showing everyone having a good time on Christmas except for Scrooge. At its crescendo, Tim had whispered to him, "See what saving your money gets you?" but Scrooge had long since stopped paying attention. These Ghosts of Christmas Past had made their point, and as usual, they really had no idea when to quit.

Back home in his bed, Scrooge didn't feel well. His knee hurt, he felt nauseous from all the waking up and going back to sleep, and his backside was sore from being kicked, *twice*. After all his hard work over the previous twelve months, the ghosts were certainly treating him a lot worse this year!

As he rubbed his rear-end, Scrooge pondered the events of the evening. He weighed what Marley had said, and then what the multiformed Ghost of Christmas Past had shown. They had certainly gone to a lot more trouble than Marley had, which had to count for something...Lying there waiting for his feet to warm up again, he really didn't know what to do. But he knew what he needed, and that was eight hours of good, refreshing, uninterrupted sleep.

STAVE FOUR.

NO REST FOR THE SAINTLY, EITHER.

FRED STOPPED at The Ball and Chain to return the "flair"; once inside, however, he realized there is no place on Earth more depressing than a prison-themed bar late on Christmas Eve, so he hurried home. Once there, he related his activities to his wife—which earned him not only dinner, but a basin of hot water, to wash the dried porridge out of his hair.

"This is wonderful!" Mrs. Fred said. "Fred, I never knew you had it in you. This is the best Christmas ever!" She put on her coat.

"Where are you going?" Fred asked.

"Over to Scrooge's, of course." Mrs. Fred got a dreamy look. "Bathing in money," she said. "How's that for a new Christmas tradition?"

This made Fred nervous; he wished to mimic the previous year in as many details as possible, and that meant letting Scrooge sleep, then awake a changed man. "Wait, dear," he said. "He's an old man. He needs his rest—I think I gave him quite a scare..."

"Wait, nothing! I want to feel the Queen's tiny metallic portrait against my nethers!" she said, and slammed the door.

Head still dripping, Fred scurried to the window. "Be careful!" he called into the cold, his voice pluming into the frigid, quiet night. "At his age, I don't know how much more Christmas Scrooge can take!"

BY THIS TIME, it was well past midnight, and while the snow had eased a bit—it too observed the holiday—the wind had not, and Mrs. Fred cursed it as she walked. But she soldiered on, warming herself with thoughts of the untold riches that were about to be poured over her until she cried, "Enough!" And she would not cry that, not ever.

Scrooge must be fantastically wealthy, she thought, otherwise why would a trio of spirits have bothered with him? Yes, the old man must've set by a staggering store of gold, in all those years of misering, she was sure of it. Even though it was only in her mind, that gold radiated as much warmth as any fire could—no amount of mud-streaked slush could quench it, nor any chill breeze beat it back. And so she walked on.

The truth was that Scrooge's year of charity had eaten away a substantial portion of his fortune. But even this would've been replaced, and more perhaps, by new money—had the activities of the counting-house not been curtailed by two forces.

The first was Bob Cratchit's sandbagging, of which I have spoken before. But the second, and just as important factor, was Scrooge's fame. With every fawning article in the press, clients left Scrooge & Marley for other firms. Even assuming that the spirits were real (and most of Scrooge's colleagues in trade did not) no hard-headed man of business could possibly trust a gentleman in the grip of...something. What if the next crop of spirits counseled less-than-sound accounting practices? Or reducing the workday from eighteen hours to a mere fourteen? Could arming the rabble be far behind?

Scrooge's colleagues at the Exchange had seen it all too often, formerly dependable sorts who, late in life, had lost their heads over some trifle—religion, a pretty young wife, pederasty—only to eventually emerge as if from a trance, sheepish and chastened. And, as often as not, stone broke.

No, no, this would not do—this Scrooge fellow had to be curtailed, before others picked up his taint. So they cut ties with Scrooge immediately, switching their commerce to other firms. Of course they applauded him publicly, and if the walls of London's clubs could talk, it would be relayed that a few even admired Scrooge—in private. But business was business, and charity was charity, and "Scroogism" (as it was now called) could not be allowed to spread.

The businessmen of London needn't have worried; even if they had given Scrooge double the business, the ex-miser's charitable activities kept him more than busy. This left the entire operation in the hands of Bob Cratchit, who was neither up to the task, nor wanted to be.

As I have said, Bob was a childlike man, and only the mute urgings of his procreative apparatus had tricked him into the role of husband and father. Just as Scrooge had drawn a lesson from the spirits' visit, Bob had drawn a complimentary one: if Scrooge was to be generous, Bob, and his whole brood, existed to provide a target for that generosity. The neatness of the arrangement proved its rightness to Bob—that, and the fact that he didn't have to work anymore. "I have always found loafing to be something I not only enjoy, but also do uncommonly well," Bob said to his ever-accepting wife. "I plan to practice this art for as many years as Scrooge has left, and more after that if possible. I am, my dear, an artist—who knows what sluggish vistas I might discover? Who knows what masterpieces of extended languor I might eventually achieve?"

Mrs. Fred passed the Cratchits' home on her way to Scrooge's apartment. Despite the lateness of the hour, their extensively renovated hovel was still brightly lit. If it had been any other house (and there hadn't been music pumping out of it), Mrs. Fred might've thought everyone inside was gainfully employed, doing needlework perhaps, or some other job whose wretched practitioners could not afford a holiday. But it being the Cratchits' place, there was a party going on, and her nature being what it was, Mrs. Fred was irresistibly drawn to it.

Not to join in, of course, nor even to scrawl "Merry Christmas!" on a slip of paper and slide it under the front door. No, what Mrs. Fred wanted—one of the few things she craved nearly as much as luxury—was feeling aggrieved, ill-used, done wrong. So Fred's wife wanted to see what Bacchic revels were taking place on Scrooge's dime. That way, she could feel morally superior, stolen from (for wasn't Scrooge's money now hers?), and entitled to gouge the irresponsible ex-miser for every last penny.

The Cratchits had not moved house. Tim's mother had a horror of "putting on airs." But as Bob's masterful leveraging of their son's sham infirmities swelled the family coffers, they had added to the original structure quite obsessively. Now, *chez Cratchit* was a vast collection of rooms outfitted with every modern convenience, encircling their rotting, rickety original quarters. The arrangement called to mind a wedding cake, with a festering rat hidden in its center.

Mrs. Cratchit insisted on living in the old, shabby part; the woman had saved and scuffled for so long that it was the only way she knew how to exist. Mrs. Cratchit was the opposite of Mrs. Fred—no increase in the family's bank balance could change her straitened world. The madness is never in the money, dear reader, but the mind.

Prosperity was not the only thing that Mrs. Cratchit ignored. She ignored the deterioration of her husband's character; she ignored the appearance of the older children in the scandal sheets; and most of all, she ignored the true nature of Tiny Tim. No matter how obvious it became that Tim was spending his days in anything but school, no matter how prodigious the boy's nefarious empire grew, or how ostentatious his ill-gotten bling became, his mother refused to acknowledge it.

Still, she was hardly the first mother to be blind to her children's faults. And we should not judge the boy himself too harshly either; without rascals, we could have no stories of redemption, and spirits would have nothing to do on holidays.

Fred's wife was not so generous to Tim as she peered into the window of the Cratchit's home. "Getting a lap dance, at his age!"

Mrs. Cratchit was knitting some scant feet away. "Tim, you haven't told me your new friend's name," Mrs. Fred heard her say. "Isn't she cold without a shirt?"

Peter Cratchit was passed out on the settee, in the thrall of something unwholesome, while the head of the household was demonstrating to the rest of their children how to use a beer-funnel. Another group (Tim's thugs, Mrs. Fred assumed) was clustered around the piano, making up dirty carols on the fly. Crippen was reading a dog-eared pamphlet entitled, "Make £££ Selling Opium to Schoolchildren." Yes, it was true—Crippen could read.

Mrs. Fred heard something; out in the yard some feet away, a bedraggled woman swore and pawed at the air, chasing spirits only she could perceive. This was a common occurence, and not just on Christmas Eve: Junkies were sprawled about the property, laying higgeldy-piggeldy like so many discharged and discarded Christmas crackers.

This, too, was Tim's doing. Over the past twelve months, so many illicit substances had been consumed in the Cratchit home, with such vigor and in such profusion, that said compounds had penetrated the very structure itself. Thanks to Tim's minions, word got around that the abode dispensed a rather sizeable "contact high," so degenerates of every stripe now hung about the property, licking it for a fee. Afterwards they tarried hollow-eyed, unable to walk, insensible to heat or cold, humans made phantoms through

The back porch of the Cratchits' home was notorious
for giving bad trips to all who licked it.

chemical submission. Mrs. Fred turned back to the window, thoroughly appalled. Within, without, wherever she looked, it was a scene authored by Scratch himself.

But the worst thing—in Mrs. Fred's eyes, at least—was the Cratchits' furniture. It was so much *nicer* than hers. And that wasn't all: the Cratchits had a piano! Beer-splashed and out-of-tune, to be sure, but a piano nevertheless. *She* didn't have a piano...And to think: these freeloaders weren't even Scrooge's flesh and blood!

"Disgusting!" Mrs. Fred said, after she'd filled her tanks, main and auxiliary, with envy and resentment. "Wait'll I tell Mr. Scrooge! That party will end, and quick!" She stomped off, double-time.

When Mrs. Fred arrived at Scrooge's apartment, she was impressed by how strongly her husband had apparently pressed the issue. Fred had smashed the lock and thrown open the door, like a barbarian sacking a citadel! No wonder Scrooge had agreed to let the money flow. Stepping over the small snow drift that had collected in the foyer, she made her way upstairs to Scrooge's chambers. Then she knocked on the door.

Scrooge lay in his bed, hoping that once tonight, ignoring something would actually cause it to go away. But his poor luck held; Fred's wife knocked again. He wrapped a pillow around his head, but Mrs. Fred would not be denied. "Mr. Scrooge!"

"Don't you ghosts ever sleep?" he cried out, throwing his pillow at the door.

"I'm not a—" Fred's wife caught herself. Though she had thought to approach Scrooge as herself, now she realized that more money might be forthcoming if her origin was supernatural. He seemed to really go for that.

"Oh, miserable man!" she said at top volume. "I have come to show you the wickedness of your ways!"

"You and everyone else," Scrooge grumbled.

Fred's wife walked into the room, and Scrooge complained about the draft.

"Get out of bed," Mrs. Fred said. "We have someplace to go, you and I. I am the Ghost of Christmas Past."

"Hah! Somebody screwed up—you lot were here an hour ago!" Scrooge rolled back over defiantly. "Go get sacked and leave me in peace."

"Oh, sorry," Mrs. Fred said. "I'm Christmas Present. I always forget."

Scrooge turned to face her, opening one eye. "You're not the Ghost of anything. You're what's-her-face, my nephew's pet shrew."

Mrs. Fred let that one go. "Ebenezer Scrooge, you have only half-learned the lesson we tried to teach. But because you are not as wicked as you one were, I have tried to be less fearsome this time. I have assumed the form of someone you know and love."

"Shows what you know," Scrooge sneered sleepily.

"Up where we are," Mrs. Fred said, "we all think she's a lovely person. She's smart, and kind, and beautiful, too. You could learn a thing or two from her, especially about how to treat your relations."

Scrooge was silent for a while. He was so very tired, and this year's crop of spirits was so very stupid. Finally, he spoke. "You're not leaving, are you?"

"Not after traveling this far, no."

Sighing heavily, Scrooge threw off the blankets. He thought this might happen, so he was fully dressed underneath. The old man swore quietly as he put on his shoes. "I suddenly understand the appeal of Judaism," he said.

"You are in the presence of a ghost, mortal!" Mrs. Fred said. "Most people would be terrified."

"Familiarity breeds contempt."

"All right, then—flattered," Fred's wife said as they went down the stairs. "How many people have spirits watching over their moral progress?"

"They're welcome to—sweet tricycling Christ!" A fresh gust of icy wind hit Scrooge's face, and he had a powerful urge to go back inside. "I really don't think this is necessary," he said to Fred's wife. "I got what the last spirit was trying to say: spread your money far and wide, give it to anybody who asks."

Mrs. Fred blanched, looking truly ghostly. "Oh, my heavens!" she said. "That is exactly the wrong message! You are so very fortunate I have come!" She grabbed his hand and began steaming towards the Cratchits at top speed. "There's something you must see."

Scrooge hung back. "How about we go back upstairs and you describe it to me?"

"No! I must show you the effects of charity without wisdom, and you of all people must see the full measure of its destruction."

Scrooge's interest in this endeavor was vanishingly small, and growing smaller with each freezing second. But Fred's wife cared deeply, and this gave her better traction in the slippery conditions. She yanked Scrooge along mercilessly.

"Scrooge, each of us plays parent to that which we bring into the world," Mrs. Fred said. "You have given much over the last year, but much you have given has ended up in the wrong hands."

"And, who, in your opinion, are the right hands?" Scrooge said. "Wait—I think I know."

"Your nephew and his wife would be an excellent choice."

"I'm getting too good at this," Scrooge said. "And where are you taking me?"

"To the Cratchits', so that you may see the effect wrongheaded charity has in this wicked world."

"Of course," Scrooge said. All at once, the entire evening made sense. "This is just too absurd. I should dump it all into the sea, just to spite you all."

"What?" the faux-ghost asked.

"'Lead on,' I said."

I can hear you now, dear reader, claiming that it would've never taken you so very long to figure out the ruse. This is easy for you to say. Remember that Scrooge had already suffered through one Christmas Eve filled with genuine apparitions. His sense of reality thus shaken, it was only logical (in a certain way), to expect that the same day a year later would be filled with even more ghosts dispensing even more lessons. Some part of Scrooge was hoping for just this occurence. Plus, his vision wasn't great. And also, there was the chronic drunkenness I mentioned before. Taken together, it makes perfect sense.

And now it was all ruined. Scrooge was terribly disappointed— last year's glimpse into eternity had been replaced by a grubby, all-too-human melee over some cash. He stopped, preparing to denounce Fred's wife right there in the snow; but then, his brain hatched a counter-plan.

THE LONGER they walked, the tighter Mrs. Fred grabbed Scrooge's hand; that comment about tossing money into the sea had spooked her, to her very core. Finally, the old man shook his bruised fingers free. "You know, for a spirit, you really leave a mark."

"Ssh!" Fred's wife said, creeping up to one of the Cratchits' windows. On tip-toe, peering over the sill, she was delighted at the scene of utter depravity. There was casual sex and loud music and gambling, but these sins were just the beginning. Everyone was using the Lord's name in vain. Crippen was slurping the fog of oblivion from a monster bong fashioned from a London bobbies' helmet. Tiny Tim was sassing his father, and pouring the contents of his pimp-cup onto the carpet. Mr. Cratchit didn't even notice, for he was busy deep-kissing someone not Tim's mother. Peter Cratchit was walking around in circles, high on patent medicines, and whipping himself for fun. The other, younger Cratchits were all naked, tattooing each other and huffing unlit gaslamps. And what was Mrs. Cratchit doing, you ask? Why, ignoring it all—and baking cookies.

Mrs. Fred motioned for Scrooge to join her. Scrooge crept over and looked inside.

"And on Christmas Eve!" Fred's wife clucked. She could hardly keep from giggling.

Scrooge put his plan into effect. "I don't see what your problem is, you old prude," he snapped. "That's just how the holiday should be celebrated. Check out the guy in the crotchless reindeer costume."

Mrs. Fred was speechless. Her jaw fell open almost as wide as Marley's had. (The real one, I mean.)

"Spirit, I want to thank you for bringing me here. I see now the error of my ways," Scrooge said. "There's only one way to dispose of my fortune: I must give it all to the Cratchits."

"But...but...that makes no sense," Mrs. Fred said. "You can't!"

"I can," Scrooge said, "and what's more, I will. You've shown me that I can't hope to untangle the conflicting wishes of the spirit world. And since my soul is already fricasseed, I might as well throw my lot in with the other sinners." He walked away.

Mrs. Fred was stunned. "Where are you going?"

"Duh," Scrooge said. "To join the party!"

"This is crazy," Fred's wife said. "You're crazy."

"If I'm crazy, then you're a figment of my imagination. *Shoo!*"

Fred's wife was completely unmanned by the situation, and began to scamper in the direction of home. Maybe Fred would know what to do.

Just in case he didn't, Scrooge tried to plant the seed. "You can tell the last ghost," he called after her, "to save his breath!"

After she'd turned the corner, Scrooge proved himself to be as good as his word: he walked right up to the Cratchits' door, and knocked. It took some real pounding to be heard over the music, but someone finally answered.

"Yeah?" Crippen said, all hooded eyes and weedy languor.

"I've come to complain about the noise," Scrooge said, pushing past. "There isn't enough of it."

Mrs. Cratchit was the first to hear Scrooge's voice, and the only one in a condition to speak coherently.

"Like what you've done to the place," Scrooge said when she appeared. "I've always been a fan of the Taj Mahal look."

"M-mister Scrooge," she said, all aflutter. "What a surprise seeing you here...at four in the morning."

"I couldn't sleep," Scrooge lied. "Ghosts had me up and down all night. No matter—is everyone here? I have an announcement that can't wait."

"I think everyone's up," Mrs. Cratchit said. The last time she'd seen Bob, he was passed out in a pool of his own sick. Happened every time he drank coconut rum.

Suddenly there was a loud laughing scream, and a woman in a thong ran between Mrs. Cratchit and Scrooge.

"That's Tiny Tim's new..." Mrs. Cratchit struggled for an appropriate word. "Governess."

"Ah."

Tim himself appeared, in hot pursuit. "Where my b—h at?" he said.

"Hello, Tim," Scrooge said. "I'm Uncle Scrooge, remember me?"

Tim didn't respond, trying to look tough. Given his size and general scrawniness, it was difficult.

"No matter," Scrooge said. He wanted to keep things moving—he suddenly had a lot to do in the hour or two of darkness that remained. "Mrs. Cratchit, please assemble your family in the parlor. I will make my announcement, then leave you to enjoy the rest of your holiday in peace."

Five minutes later, Scrooge stood in front of a semi-comatose Cratchit clan, surrounded by their equally impaired servants, retainers, and general hangers-on. "After the events of this evening," Scrooge said, "the details of which I will not bore you with—"

"More ghosts?" Crippen said mid-inhale, thinking their earlier gambit had worked.

"Yes, more ghosts," Scrooge said, then continued. "I have decided to give all my money to my sole heir, my nephew Fred and his wife, Shrewtastic."

Everyone sprang to life. Crippen moved toward Scrooge with murderous intent; in the right hands, a bong can be lethal. Scrooge saw the look in his eye and said, "That won't do you any good—I've already made out my will." Scrooge looked at each person in turn—Bob, Mrs. Cratchit, Tim. "Do any of you have questions?"

"But...*why?*" Bob asked, hurt.

"You have got to be kidding," Scrooge said. Stepping over a

conatose reveler, he walked towards the door. "Also, Bob," Scrooge added, "you're sacked. Merry Christmas!"

"Tell me the engraver didn't f--k
up my name," Scrooge said.

STAVE FIVE.

———·———

TIM'S SECRET.

As soon as the door closed behind Scrooge, Tiny Tim declared, "I'm gonna bust a cap in that guy."

"What good will that do?" Mrs. Cratchit was distraught. This was something she couldn't ignore, and while it was all well and good to deny prosperity, she'd gotten used to the privilege. "He's already done a will."

"Wills can be changed," Tim said. "Right, Mr. Ligature?"

An older man sat up from the couch, dislodging an aspiring actress. Years ago, he had looked distinguished, but now he just looked seedy. "Indubitably, Master T."

"Dry your tears, mother," Tim commanded. "Father, put down that straight razor. Liggy here is one of London's preeminent forgers. He did a fake will for our savior Jesus Christ—and it stood up in court, too."

"But will I have to get rid of my sundries-girl?" Mrs. Cratchit's one luxury was a servant whose job it was to walk besides her from morning until night, wearing a lumpy garment which contained every conceivable household item. The poor thing resembled a sweaty potato.

"No, mother," Tim said. "No one is getting fired tonight, or any other night. Mr. Ligature," he said, "start writing. 'I, Ebenezer Scrooge, being of sound mind and body…'"

Meanwhile, some distance away, Fred and his bride were similarly shocked by the turn the evening had taken.

"Fred, you've got to *do* something," Mrs. Fred demanded.

"What would you suggest I do?" Fred replied. "The old goat's made up his mind."

"Well, make him unmake it," she said. "You're his flesh and blood."

"Quit saying that." Fred had broken out something strong, and was taking generous pulls from it. "Seems to me that everything was okay," he said, "until a certain person got involved."

"Oh, you shouldn't've said that," Mrs. Fred said, her voice menacing and low. "That's another year of celibacy for you."

Fred took another gulp. "Who says I've been celibate?"

Normally this would've earned him a session with the thimble, but his wife had bigger issues to attend to (and he was out of range). "Please, Fred," she asked, "go talk to him. You'll be able to convince him. He likes you."

"It's still dark out," Fred said. "I'll do it tomorrow."

"No!" Fred's wife said. She reached into a drawer, and pulled out a piece of paper. "Go over there right now, and show Scrooge this!" It was Scrooge's last will, which named Fred his sole heir. "You tell him we'll fight! We'll say he was insane—that Christmas Eve always makes him insane!" Fred's wife let that sink in, but it had no effect, so she changed direction.

"Tell you what. If you go now, I'll have something waiting for you when you come back. Something you haven't had in a very, very long time..."

Fred was officially over Mrs. Fred. "I'd prefer breakfast." He grabbed a fresh bottle, and left.

WHEN SCROOGE returned home, he headed directly for his bed. But not to sleep.

Instead, he took the bronze bust from the Prince of Wales, and some pillows, and arranged them to look like his sleeping form. It was passably realistic, with the gaslamps turned down low.

"That'll do," Scrooge said brightly. "After all, we're not dealing with geniuses." Chuckling at the mayhem he was about to cause, he took some of his counterfeit money—collecting it had been his only hobby, before the spirits had come along—and threw it into a sack. Just as he placed the sack by the door, he heard someone entering downstairs. "Whoop! Hallo!" Suddenly Scrooge felt wonderful; he should mess with people more often, it did wonders for his mood. The ex-miser had just enough time to leap into the fireplace and shimmy up the chimney. Bracing his feet on two protruding bricks, he perched there like a deranged vulture, just out of sight.

A moment later, Fred stuck his head through the door. "Uncle?"

There was no answer, so Fred walked over to the bed, and sat on its edge. "Uncle, it's me, Fred."

Fred was quite fantastically drunk; Scrooge could smell his breath from inside the chimney.

Over on the bed, Fred was getting worried. The shape wasn't moving. "Uncle?" he said uncertainly, then reached out a finger and gave the shape a poke. He drew back; it was cold, as cold as the grave.

"FRED!" Scrooge shouted from the chimney.

The old man timed his moment well; Fred was so startled he fell off the bed. When Scrooge heard him hit the floor, it was all he could do not to laugh.

"U-uncle?"

"I *was* your uncle," Scrooge intoned, pleased at how the chimney gave his voice a nice eerie echo. "Now, I have gone over to the other side. I'm dead, Fred—and without my reclamation completed!" To emphasize this last point, Scrooge gave a wail.

"But that can't be so!" Fred said, terrified. "Think of all the people you helped!"

"Not enough! Not enough!" Scrooge said. "Only the worthy ones counted! Perhaps if I hadn't been constantly distracted by your deceitfulness—I knew about your Italian Escape Fund, and your wife's badgering...But no!" Scrooge was actually freaking himself out a little. "You—and your wife—have condemned me to H—l!"

"Oh god! Oh god! Save me!" Fred said, cowering. He'd never quite believed his Uncle about the spirits, but now he had no doubt. "What can I do?"

"Nothing!" Scrooge said. "You must live with the knowledge you hindered a good man—your flesh and blood—and sent him to eternal torment."

Fred brought his head from the floor. "Now, Uncle, be fair—you weren't that good. At the end there, I'll admit you were a prince, but before then? A grade-A s—theel."

"How dare you disrespect the dead!" Scrooge moaned. "Sa-a-ay you're sorry!"

"I won't. It's the truth."

"Gee," Scrooge said, "that's too bad. I was going to give you that sackful of money by the door. Just to show there are no hard feelings."

"Really?"

"Yes, really! My time here is short, but I must tell you one more thing—"

"Uncle, why can't I see you?" Fred asked. "You could see *your* ghosts, right?"

"Didn't I just tell you my time was short?" Scrooge said crossly. "Don't waste it with a bunch of stupid questions!...Fred, listen to me: it's not too late for you—you can still change. Go get a job. Lay off the sauce. And for God's sake, divorce your wife!"

"I don't much like the first idea," Fred said, "nor the second. But I must admit the third one has real merit." Between the liquor, and the forced celibacy, he was horny enough to r—e Scrooge's bust. "We haven't had sex in years."

"**TOO MUCH INFORMATION!**" Scrooge's voice boomed.

"'member when you gave me a hundred pounds to establish a free bunion clinic?" Fred said. "That was the last time."

"**NOT LISTENING! NOT LISTENING!**" Scrooge said, making a loud humming noise. Then Scrooge stopped. "You pushed me too far, Fred. I've just put a curse on that money."

"Hey!" Fred said. "Why'd you do that? I was going to spend it."

"Too late now," Scrooge said. "Give it to your wife. Tell her to spend it. Bad things will happen, I promise."

Fred chuckled at the prospect of causing his wife grief. "Well, that's better than nothing, I guess."

"Now, GO!" Scrooge boomed, making Fred's laughter catch in his throat.

"Uncle…?" Fred ventured quietly. "About your will…"

"GO!" Scrooge said. "**LEAVE THIS PLACE, AND SPONGE NO MORE!**"

The effort of this made Scrooge cough a bit, but he was able to hold it until after his nephew had scurried downstairs, clutching the bagful of counterfeit money.

TEN MINUTES LATER as he was making up another bag, Scrooge heard Crippen and Tiny Tim talking at the bottom of the stairs.

"Aren't you coming with?" Crippen said.

"Only if you carry me on your shoulders."

"Get stuffed, farter."

Ten seconds later, the weedy manservant burst through the door to Scrooge's bedroom. "Get up, Scrooge!" he yelled. "I'm the Ghost of Kicking Your A—e!"

Crippen saw the shape on the bed, and rushed towards it. But before he could swing his sand-filled sock, Scrooge's voice boomed from the chimney.

"**STOP, EVIL MAN!**"

Crippen stopped, all right. He stood there, flabbergasted.

"Who's that? If anybody's hiding up here, they better come out or I'll—"

"You cannot reach me where I am," Scrooge said, "nor can you harm me any longer. I am dead, Crippen. You're speaking to Ebenezer Scrooge's ghost."

Crippen, like most criminals, was a bully; but given his pitiful physique, the prospect of facing something more powerful than a seven-year-old child made him distinctly uneasy. Furthermore, all the lousy things he had done gave Crippen a lively sense of guilt and dread; this, too, was an occupational hazard. Both factors now spewed forth, mixing to form abject terror.

Uttering a wordless cry, Crippen turned and ran—but not before grabbing the sack of coin Scrooge had very thoughtfully put by the door.

After Crippen had pounded down the stairs, Scrooge wriggled

his way down the chimney. Lucky Crippen was such a scaredy cat, Scrooge thought, as he removed the bust and pillow. Outside the sky was lightening, and with every passing moment, his ruse looked more fake.

"So, did you plant the will?" Tiny Tim asked, as Crippen stood there panting on the stoop.

"I forgot."

"Well, go back up, then," Tiny Tim piped menacingly.

Crippen shook his head emphatically. "Your Uncle's dead, and his ghost is up there!"

"Bulls—t!" Tiny Tim reached up and swiped the crumpled will from Crippen's hand. "Gimme that. And that m—rf—r isn't my Uncle!"

Monkey-quick and as sure as a dancer, Tim climbed the stairs, taking care that no one saw how easily he did so. When he reached the door to his Uncle's chambers, his manner transformed itself—his usual swagger was gone, replaced by a kind of dew-eyed self-abasing forelock-tugging that only can be properly described as "emetic."

"Good morning, Mr. Scrooge!" Tim knocked on the door politely. "I've come to wish you a Merry Christmas!"

"Come in."

Scrooge didn't sound like a ghost, nor look like one either. That superstitious idiot, Tim thought, making a mental note to sack Crippen. But he'd do it after the first of the year—there were tax advantages.

The old man was sitting on the edge of his bed. "Come closer, my boy," he said warmly. He patted the bed. "Over here, by me."

All smiles, Tim hobbled over.

"Did you make it up those stairs *all by yourself?*"

"I did, Mr. Scrooge," Tim said. "That's how much I wanted to wish you a Merry Christmas."

"That's awfully kind of you, Tim," Scrooge said. "Come closer, so I can see you more clearly. These old eyes, like the rest of me, are frail. And the light is weak yet; the world is still asleep."

"Why do you have a hairbrush, Mr. Scrooge? You only have old man's fringe."

"Hairbrushes have other uses, too, Tim!" Quick as a flash, the old man grabbed the deceitful urchin. Tim tried to struggle, but a year's worth of vitamin-free dissolution had made him as weak as an early morning breeze. Scrooge had no trouble laying Tim crosswise across his lap. Rolling up a sleeve, he began to spank Tiny Tim vigorously.

"You've had this coming for twelve months, you rascal! I was too indulgent with you, but now the scales will be balanced!...Steal people's clothes, will you? Pretend to be a spirit, eh?...Girls in thongs? Didn't think I knew about lap-dancing, did you?...Go ahead, call me foul names, you poisonous little twerp!"

Pants-on spanking was good, but Scrooge wanted more. He ripped down the boy's trousers, exposing his bare b—m. There, tattooed across the boy's backside one word per cheek, was the following:

Thug Life.

Scrooge was appalled. "Tim, you should be ashamed of yourself! Your mother must be so disappointed in you. I know"—Scrooge feigned a bright idea—"shall we see if I can remove that by hand? I don't know if it can be done, but let's try."

Scrooge whaled and whopped, until Tim's bottom was too red to make out the words. Pleased with his work, he let the sobbing mini-kingpin slide to the floor. Mumbling swears, the crying boy pulled up his baggy prison-styled trousers, and snuffled his snotty nose.

"Don't you *dare* wipe your nose on my sheets."

Defiant, Tim moved to do just that, but Scrooge lunged at him. "Boo!" Scrooge said.

"Ahhh!" Tiny Tim screamed, then scrambled towards the door. He paused once, to make a threat, but Scrooge lunged again and sent him running even faster.

Scrooge watched as Tim scuttled down the stairs, well and truly "crippled" by a manually savaged seat. The old ex-miser chuckled to himself, "God bless us, every b-m!"

CODA.

HAPPILY EVER AFTER?

Scrooge had never trusted banks; so he spent a lovely Christmas morning digging up all the coins he'd buried under the waiting room then decanting them into steamer trunks. In the afternoon, after signing over the insurance to a local orphanage, he hired a few neighbor kids to put the torch to his old counting-house. They enjoyed it, and so did he.

By sunset, Scrooge was on a boat bound for the Continent, with more baggage than anyone had ever seen. This contained his entire remaining wealth, a considerable but not outlandish sum. The ex-miser had a propensity for seasickness, but this was more than counteracted by happy thoughts of his heirs—whoever the courts decided they were—being soundly and irrevocably screwed.

Scrooge's first stop was Switzerland, where his luggage went directly into a numbered bank account. Then, as all free spirits do, he felt himself drawn to Paris, where he planned to spend the balance of his days, kind, generous, anonymous, and happy.

Scrooge discovered that a year's worth of funding deadbeats had curtailed his guilt quite nicely. From now on, the old man had decided, he would tithe; let the Church puzzle out the wishes of the hereafter (and let *them* burn if they were wrong!). Scrooge had done his bit, and would do more, but now it was time for him to really live.

Thus that Michaelmas found our hero tucked away in a cozy bistro, eating delicious food and flirting with an attractive barmaid. A slight improvement from The Ball and Chain, Scrooge thought.

After the meal was over, Scrooge dallied, as was his new custom. He drank a cognac, and pondered the meaning of it all. "A life spent in service to others," he said quietly to himself, "is only as good as the others you serve."

A man at the table closest to Scrooge took note. "Are you a philosopher?" he asked.

"No, no," Scrooge said with a smile. "Just someone trying to figure out this world."

"If you find the answer," the man teased, "let me know."

The drink and the man's genial nature loosened Scrooge's tongue, and he told the stranger his entire story, from Marley's first visit to the affair with Tim's b—m.

"Bravo!" the man said, when Scrooge told him about spanking Tim. "What a little ratfink."

"You can't blame him, I suppose," Scrooge said with a sigh. "He's only a product of our times. Or perhaps he *is* a ratfink...After everything that's happened, I admit I'm more confused than ever. As long as man measures himself by what he *has* instead of what he *is*, charity is doomed to piddle along, a weak flowing trickle in such a thirsty world. Say what you will, friend: a man will not do anything contrary to his interests for long—even if you threaten him with everlasting torment."

"You know," the man said, "you might be interested in some ideas I've come up with, ways to solve just these problems, and make a better world."

"I'm all ears," Scrooge said.

The man—who was all beard—looked at him puzzledly.

"It means 'I'm listening.'"

"My name is Karl Marx," the man said, digging a coffee-stained brochure out of his pocket and handing it to Scrooge. The ex-miser listened politely as Mr. Marx began a long discourse about something he called "communism," and how it was destined to change the world.

To Scrooge—especially after the events of the last weeks—it seemed like a nice theory that would never work; but he was not so boorish to tell his new friend that. After about an hour, simply to get out of the conversation, Scrooge gave the man a donation.

"Thank you, Comrade Scrooge," Mr. Marx said, as they parted. "We will remember this, come the Revolution."

"Most assuredly," Scrooge said, not convinced. Still, the old man walked to his hotel pleased at his good deed. Comrade Marx's heart seemed to be in the right place...and after all, what harm could it possibly do?

FA-LA-LA.

As always, thanks to the braintrust—Kate, Edward and Jon—and to Mom for reading the real thing to me one Christmas Eve so many years ago.

This book has been designed to recall the original edition of *A Christmas Carol*, produced in December 1843. All illustrations, except for "Whiskerando" on the title page, are taken from that edition. (Also by John Leech, that one is from an issue of *Punch* published in 1851.)

Additional copies of this book—or any of my other books, read 'em all at one sitting and you win a free steak—may be ordered via online bookseller, your local bookstore, or at my website, mikegerber.com. Stop by and say "Whoop! Hallo!"

Printed in the United States
130850LV00004B/5/P